ONE POT SUPREME

One Pot
SUPREME

The Complete Cookbook for Skillets, Slow Cookers, Sheet Pans, and More!

GWYN NOVAK

PHOTOGRAPHY BY HÉLÈNE DUJARDIN

ROCKRIDGE
PRESS

For general information on our other products and services or to obtain technical support, please contact our Customer Care Department within the United States at (866) 744-2665, or outside the United States at (510) 253-0500.

Rockridge Press publishes its books in a variety of electronic and print formats. Some content that appears in print may not be available in electronic books, and vice versa.

TRADEMARKS: Rockridge Press and the Rockridge Press logo are trademarks or registered trademarks of Callisto Media Inc. and/or its affiliates, in the United States and other countries, and may not be used without written permission. All other trademarks are the property of their respective owners. Rockridge Press is not associated with any product or vendor mentioned in this book.

Interior and Cover Designer: Mando Daniel

Art Producer: Hannah Dickerson

Editor: Lauren Ladoceour

Production Editor: Ruth Sakata Corley

Photography © 2020 Hélène Dujardin, food styling by Anna Hampton. All illustrations used under license from Shutterstock.com and iStock.com.

ISBN: Print 978-1-64739-005-1 | eBook 978-1-64739-006-8

R0

To everyone who wants to eat better in less time

Contents

Introduction

I've been a professional chef and cooking instructor for the past 25 years, and I love teaching people how to cook. But when I'm done at the end of a busy day, the last thing I feel like doing is making dinner for my family. Thank goodness for one-pot meals—food that only needs one dish, pan, or pot.

When people hear the phrase "one-pot cooking," they often think of hours of slow cooking in a Crock-Pot as winter snow falls. While that's fabulous and delicious, one-pot cooking is so much more than that. In fact, at times it can be just the opposite, allowing you to get dinner on the table in less than 30 minutes.

I'm also a big proponent of seasonal eating. In other words, using what's in season to create delicious, easy meals. But I don't like overly involved recipes with tons of ingredients. I honestly believe that if you use what's fresh and in season, your cooking automatically improves. Let the ingredients speak for themselves. A little splash of olive oil, a sprinkle of kosher salt, and a grind of black pepper are often all you need to let them sing.

In this book, we'll walk you through each season of the year (spring, summer, fall, and winter) and show you how to use a variety of cookware you probably already have to make the most of those seasonal treasures. From sheet pans, skillets, and stockpots to baking dishes, Dutch ovens, sauté pans, and slow cookers, this book aims to give you ideas for delicious and oh-so-practical meals throughout the year—and, of course, we couldn't leave out the ever-popular electric pressure cooker. Also, just in case you don't have the pot or pan a recipe calls for, there are tips on how to adapt the recipes for the one you do have.

Rest assured, this cookbook sticks to the rules of one-pot cooking. I promise you: You're not going to have a stack of dishes to wash when it's all said and done. While I love to cook, I really dislike the cleanup, and I'm guessing the same is true for you as well. The less we have to clean, the better!

With everything in one pot or pan, you might even get a little time back in your life. That's one of the big benefits of seasonal cooking. One-pot dishes can (and will!) taste extraordinary. With this abundance of recipes as your guide and different seasons' bounty as your inspiration, you'll be sure to find an appealing dish to fit whatever you need at the moment, no matter what the day brings. What do you say, want to give it a try? You have nothing to lose and everything to gain!

Everything One Pot

Our lives are busier than ever. After working all day and taking care of the kids, the last thing most of us want to do by the time we get home is figure out what to eat, much less make it and then clean up. That's where one-pot meals come in—minimal mess and dinner on the table in a fraction of the time. Who couldn't use more of that?

The One-Pot Promise

If you had only one pot or pan to cook in on a deserted island, what would you make? Perhaps that sounds limiting at first, but the truth is that one-pot cookery comes with an inspiring set of possibilities—and with minimal effort and fantastic results. The only recipes you'll find here are ones that are truly one-pot dishes. It's so frustrating to start preparing what is touted as a one-pot meal, only to have to pull out three other pots and pans to get dinner on the table. This isn't to say you won't need a cutting board or a lone mixing bowl on occasion, but it will be minimal. The recipes you'll find here—among my favorites are the Savory Beef Stew (page 191), Pulled Pork Sandwiches (page 197), and Chipotle Bean Burritos (page 139)—are all about cooking an entire meal in one piece of cookware from start to finish. Absolutely. You won't need to wash the pot in between. I created these recipes with two things in mind: freeing you from an overload of work and dirty dishes and providing you with an abundance of delicious seasonal recipes.

But what if you don't have, say, an electric pressure cooker to make Baby Back Ribs (page 120)? Not to worry. No matter what pot or cookware you have on hand or what skill level you're at when it comes to cooking, you will be able to use and enjoy the adaptation tips and recipes in this book.

We'll be cooking with a variety of one-pot cookware, but don't feel that you have to run out and get them all. Most of these recipes can be adapted easily to another vessel you do have on hand. For instance, a soup traditionally prepared in a stockpot can be done in a Crock-Pot, Dutch oven, or pressure cooker. The same is true of sheet pans, baking dishes, and even large skillets and sauté pans. Just because a recipe employs a particular vessel, doesn't mean it is to be used exclusively for that recipe. Once you really delve into one-pot cooking, you'll quickly start to feel more comfortable interchanging pots. That's because one-pot cooking is as practical as it is delicious. What could be better than that?

Favorite (One) Pots and Pans

From cheesy baked pastas to succulent pulled pork sandwiches, there's a way to make them in an all-in-one pot or pan. Call it "streamlined cooking" or "self-contained meals": It's all possible thanks to these versatile pieces of cookware.

Oven-Safe Skillet

A skillet is a pan with a handle and sloped sides. It is meant to be used on your stovetop and, if oven-safe, transferred to the oven to finish cooking. It's ideal for dishes that you will sear, stir-fry, or sauté or for when you are cooking foods over high heat, such as pan-seared steaks or sandwiches. They come in a variety of sizes, but the most common and useful are 8-, 10-, and 12-inch skillets. If you are just cooking for two people, an 8-inch will be fine for most dishes. But if you're regularly cooking for four or more people, definitely opt for a 10- or 12-inch pan. Any larger than that, and it becomes too heavy to work with.

WHAT IT CAN DO

One of the biggest benefits of an oven-safe skillet (meaning the handle is not plastic and will not melt) is that it can go from the stovetop directly into the oven. This is invaluable as it allows you to brown meats in the skillet on the stovetop and finish them in the oven. This prevents them from burning on the outside before they're fully cooked on the inside.

WHY IT'S VERSATILE

A skillet is a versatile vessel to cook with, as it can conveniently take the place of a baking dish when needed. Just be sure it's large enough to fit all of your ingredients without crowding them, otherwise they won't roast. If items are too close together in the pan, they will steam instead of roast and you won't get the nice brown exterior you're looking for. That crust is where all of the flavor is!

COOKING TIP

Make sure the pan and the oil you use to cook with are good and hot. If not, the proteins or vegetables you add to the skillet will absorb the fat, resulting in a heavy, fatty dish. So be a little patient. Also, if you finish the dish in the oven, be sure to place an oven mitt over the handle of the skillet when it comes out of the oven. It's easy to forget that the pan is still extremely hot.

CLEANUP

For the longevity of your skillet, don't rinse it with cold water as soon as it comes off the hot stove. Warm or hot water is fine, but the extreme difference in temperatures with cold water can cause your pan to warp. Instead, let it cool off for a bit and place it in the sink with hot water and dish soap until you're ready to get to it after dinner. It will clean much more easily. If you have really burned the bottom of your pan, fill it with hot soapy water and a dryer sheet, like the kind you add to your laundry. Let it sit for a few hours, overnight if necessary, and that stubborn stain will be much easier to clean.

Sauté Pan with Cover

People often confuse a sauté pan with a skillet because, in fact, they are very similar. The big difference is that a sauté pan has straight sides (rather than the sloped sides of a skillet) and often comes with a lid or cover. Because of its straight sides, it has a slightly larger bottom than a skillet. It's primarily used for stovetop cooking, but it can also transition to the oven when needed. It's the perfect vessel for searing meat and making pan sauces. When it comes to choosing a size for your new sauté pan, follow the same guidelines as for skillets above.

WHAT IT CAN DO

Just like the skillet, a sauté pan is wonderful because it can go straight from a hot burner to a hot oven, assuming the handles are made of metal. With a tight-fitting lid, it's also a great choice for making grain entrees such as a chicken-rice pilaf, which needs to be covered in order to absorb the cooking liquid. Uncovered, it's also the perfect vessel to make risotto, as it has a wide, flat bottom that yields a lot of surface area for the rice to absorb the stock.

WHY IT'S VERSATILE

As previously mentioned, a large sauté pan can always stand in for a skillet, but did you know it can also double as a baking dish when necessary? Just remember: Don't crowd the pan to prevent steaming, and be sure to leave the lid off so the food will beautifully roast.

COOKING TIP

While a sauté pan and a skillet can often be used interchangeably, opt for the sauté pan if you're making a dish that has a considerable amount of liquid in it. The straight sides will help prevent the liquid from sloshing out of the pan and onto your stovetop, resulting in less to clean up in the end!

CLEANUP

Because you're typically working with high heat with a sauté pan, don't let it sit around too long after dinner. It will be much harder to get any burned-on bits off. Instead, fill it with about ½ inch of hot water and a generous squirt of dish detergent and leave it until after the meal. It will clean quickly and easily. If you do have some stubborn bits that don't want to break loose, empty the pan, put a fresh ½ inch of water in it, place it over high heat, and they'll be gone in no time.

Baking Dish

A baking dish is an oven-proof rectangular vessel that is perfect for anything from casseroles and enchiladas to potato skins and poppers. Typically 9 by 13 inches, it is available in a variety of materials: glass, ceramic, and enamel-covered stoneware being the most common. What you choose is really up to you, your budget, and overall style. Its true appeal is that it can go from freezer to oven to table to fridge and look great doing it!

WHAT IT CAN DO

When choosing a baking dish, most people go by appearance, but keep in mind that you also want a dish that has large, easy-to-grip handles. The last thing you want when you're pulling the dish out of the hot oven with bulky mitts on is to lose your grasp and have an entire lasagna fall to the floor.

WHY IT'S VERSATILE

If you're short on roasting or sheet pans and you don't have a lot to cook, a baking dish can easily pinch-hit. With high sides like a roasting pan and built to sustain high heat, it's an obvious substitute that is perfect for roasting meats, such as a whole chicken or a small roast beef.

COOKING TIP

If you opt for a glass baking pan, which is the most reasonably priced, just be sure to read the manufacturer's guidelines. Unlike the other materials, glass does not perform as well when it goes from one extreme temperature to another (such as from a cold refrigerator to a hot oven). It could crack or shatter if not properly handled.

CLEANUP

Baking dishes spend a lot of time in a hot oven, and as a result, they are going to have some crusty baked-on, caked-on spots to scrub off. The best thing to do is give yourself a fighting chance by placing the dish in a sink filled with hot soapy water. Then, when you're done with dinner, attack it with a soft scrubber, one that won't scratch the surface of your dish. Wrapping a thick paper towel around the head of a wooden spoon and scraping away also works well. It's also possible to use one of the mesh bags onions and lemons come in: Fill it with a sponge, tie up the end and you have your very own homemade pot scrubber.

Sheet Pan

A sheet pan is a large, rectangular metal pan that is intended to be used in the oven. The size most home cooks use (13 by 18 inches) has raised sides that are about 1-inch high. These pans are perfect for roasting vegetables, making pizzas, and of course, the myriad of sheet-pan dinners you'll find throughout this book.

WHAT IT CAN DO

When roasting foods on a sheet pan, you want to be careful not to overcrowd them. In other words, you don't want the foods to touch, causing them to steam rather than roast. Give them a little elbow room (plus a lot of heat and some time!) and they will brown to perfection.

WHY IT'S VERSATILE

Sheet pans can be used much like a baking dish. Their straight metal sides, while not overly high, will help keep the food on the pan. Just be sure to purchase a heavy enough sheet pan that it won't warp in the oven when exposed to high heat. If it does warp, none of your food will cook properly.

COOKING TIP
To really get great browning (caramelization) on your food, preheat your sheet pan. Simply place it in the oven empty (with no food on it) as the oven is coming up to temperature. When the oven is hot enough, place the food on the pan. You should hear a sizzling sound. Every five minutes or so, give the pan a shake to help the food cook evenly and brown nicely.

CLEANUP
The easiest way to clean a sheet pan is to prevent the mess in the first place. You can do this by lining it with a piece of parchment paper. Similar to wax paper but without the wax, parchment paper is stick-resistant and heat-tolerant up to 500°F. When you're finished cooking, simply wad it up and throw it away! You'll still need to wipe the pan clean, but it won't be nearly as onerous a task as without the parchment. Do yourself a favor and buy it by the case! Note: Wax paper will smoke and may ignite if used in the oven.

Stockpot

A stockpot is a flat-bottomed metal pot with high, straight sides, a wide opening, handles, and a lid with a handle on top. It's perfect for making soups and stocks, as well as for cooking pastas and steaming shellfish, to name just a few uses.

WHAT IT CAN DO
Stockpots are large cooking vessels and are fabulous because you can cook large quantities of food in them all at one time, rather than needing a variety of pots. They are designed to be used on the stovetop indoors, but they are also great to have on hand for the holidays when you want to fry your turkey outdoors.

WHY IT'S VERSATILE
Stockpots are incredibly versatile because they come in such an array of sizes. There are no standard sizes when it comes to stockpots. Choose a heavy one that won't warp and will hold all of your food, but one that you can still pick up when it is full and hot.

Since stockpots come in a variety of sizes, choose one that is in line with the amount of food you typically cook. If you're making a soup recipe that calls for just 4 servings, you don't need a 20-quart stockpot. Most recipes (including everything in this book) can be made in an 8- to 12-quart pot. Additionally, use the lid that came with it for quicker cooking. Covered foods cook more quickly.

CLEANUP

Like the other vessels we have discussed, as soon as you are finished with the pot, place it in the sink and fill it with hot soapy water. Then drain it and refill with hot water and soap, and cleanup should be a breeze. If you do have tougher bits to remove, it's okay to use a more abrasive scrubber such as steel wool on your stockpots. Don't have steel wool and need it clean immediately? Crumple up a sheet of aluminum foil and use that to scrub your pot. It can take it.

Dutch Oven

If there is one pot you really can't do without in your kitchen, it's the Dutch oven. A thick, heavy pot typically made of cast iron, this workhorse is best suited for braising large, tougher cuts of meat in liquids at low temperatures for a long period of time. It is designed to go from the stovetop to the oven, and it's even beautiful enough to go straight to the table. It is, however, an investment so you want to be sure to pick the right one. For most people that will be a 5- to 7-quart Dutch oven. With that, you'll easily be able to create dishes for 4 to 6 servings. You also have the option of a round or oval shape. Both are beautiful, but if you're doing a lot of stovetop cooking with it, you might want to opt for the round. It fits better on the burner.

WHAT IT CAN DO

Long before the all-in-one pots came along, there was the Dutch oven. Because of its design, you can sauté as well as stew in it. The tight-fitting lid with a handle on top is ideal for keeping in all of the heat, perfect for long braises.

WHY IT'S VERSATILE

Dutch ovens were meant for low-and-slow cooking, but with their high sides they also make the perfect vessel for deep-frying. Give making fried chicken a try in it. Remove the lid, and they are equally good as a substitute for a baking dish. They'll even step in for a sauté pan or skillet, if needed.

COOKING TIP

While these beasts are one of the best vessels in your arsenal, you do need to be careful when you're lifting them. They are heavy enough on their own, but when you add in boiling hot liquids, you have a recipe for a big burn—so be careful when removing them from the oven.

CLEANUP

After braising in the oven for hours at a time, you would imagine that an enamel-coated Dutch oven would be a bear to clean, but it's actually easy. Simply place it in the sink and fill it with hot soapy water. When you are ready to clean it, all you need to do is drain the water and wipe it clean. Over time, however, the inside of the pot will stain. You can get rid of those nasty stains by filling it with warm water and 1 teaspoon bleach for every quart of water you add. Cover and let the Dutch oven sit overnight, and it will be almost like new in the morning.

Slow Cooker

A slow cooker, sometimes known as a Crock-Pot, is a freestanding appliance that cooks food at a low and steady temperature. It's the ultimate in hands-off cooking. As it requires hours for the meal to cook, you do have to plan ahead a bit, but it's well worth the minimal effort when you walk into the house and are enveloped by the aromas of dinner waiting for you. It's perfect for chili or beef stew—and even some surprising dishes like macaroni and cheese or spaghetti and meatballs. Because they are reasonably priced (compared to a Dutch oven), many people have a few different-size slow cookers. For dips, a 1½- to 2-quart model is perfect. But if you're making dinner for four to six people, you really want to invest in a 5- to 6-quart slow cooker.

WHAT IT CAN DO

Most slow cookers have two settings: high and low. The high temperature usually cooks at around 212°F, while the low hovers just above 200°F. Many also feature a warm setting (165°F). This safely keeps food warm without overcooking it.

WHY IT'S VERSATILE

Many of the newer slow cookers now offer some of the same features as an electric pressure cooker. If you're in the market, consider opting for one with those bells and whistles—you'll eliminate one less kitchen appliance in your pantry.

COOKING TIP

Slow cookers are really great at taking inexpensive cuts of meat and tenderizing them while they cook for hours, thereby saving you a bit of money on food. The other huge benefit of hours of cooking is that the flavor intensifies, so "set it and forget it!" You'll be richly rewarded in the end. Also, when you convert a regular recipe into one for your slow cooker, remember to reduce the liquid by about one-third.

CLEANUP

Slow cookers are notoriously difficult to clean. As you can imagine, after hours of cooking, there's usually a tough-to-remove ring around the inside of the pot. You can purchase liners for your slow cooker, or you can simply spray it with cooking spray before each use. You can also fill it with water, a healthy splash of vinegar, and 1 tablespoon baking soda. Turn it on, and it will do most of the cleaning for you.

Electric Pressure Cooker

An electric pressure cooker is a countertop appliance that does the job of a slow cooker, rice cooker, steamer, sous vide bath, yogurt maker, sauté pan, warming pot, and, of course, a pressure cooker. It's a single appliance that does the job of seven different kitchen appliances or tools. Want succulent pork chops for dinner in no time? An electric pressure cooker is your go-to appliance. It's also great for short ribs and soups. Like everything else, these come in a variety of sizes. Generally, if you are cooking for three to five people, definitely consider a 5- to 7-quart electric pressure cooker.

WHAT IT CAN DO

The really great benefit of an electric pressure cooker is its ability to allow you to sauté directly in the same pot in which you will pressure cook, making it the perfect one-pot vessel. No more sauté pan followed by a slow cooker; it can all be done in one pot. The other great thing is that you can create sumptuous dishes in a fraction of the time. Dishes that you would normally reserve for the weekends can be on the table in an hour on a weeknight with the help of a pressure cooker.

WHY IT'S VERSATILE

It is no exaggeration to say that these vessels really do take the place of seven different pieces of kitchen equipment. The sauté feature of the pressure cooker can stand in for a sauté pan or skillet if needed, while the low and slow necessary to cook in a Dutch oven or slow cooker can be sped up in the pressure cooker. It really is the most versatile pot you'll own.

COOKING TIP

While the pressure cooker will cook the food in a compressed amount of time, keep in mind that it does require time to both pressurize before it begins cooking the food and depressurize after cooking is complete. Depending on your cooker, this could add 15 minutes to each end. But that's hands-off time for you.

CLEANUP

Because there is so much moisture in the pressure cooker, they are relatively easy to clean up. Often all they require is a little hot soapy water and a sponge to get them sparkly clean again. If you do have some pesky browned bits you want to get rid of, keep a can of Bar Keepers Friend on hand. It's a great product that cleans just about anything.

QUICK KITCHEN-
COUNTER POINTS

What's more appealing than a great meal made with a single piece of cookware—one that's low on prep and stress with these streamlining tips:

1. Keep jarred or bottled sauces, frozen piecrusts, and pizza crusts on hand all the time. You never know when the mood will strike!

2. Really don't like to prep your vegetables? Shop the salad bar at your store or take advantage of precut veggies (such as cubed butternut squash and zucchini noodles) in the produce section.

3. Measure out and prep all your ingredients before you start cooking. It will go much more quickly and be much less stressful.

4. Quick tip: Thinly sliced or diced proteins will cook faster than larger cuts.

5. If you're cooking whole vegetables, remember that smaller, baby vegetables are more tender and will cook more quickly.

6. When you're roasting or baking, use the convection setting (if you have one) on your oven. By engaging the fan, it will cook your food more quickly and evenly.

7. One-pot cooking is amazing, but full disclosure: It precludes sides of grains like quinoa and rice, since those typically call for another pot. Consider buying microwaveable grains if you know someone at the table will miss them.

Cooking Through the Seasons

The recipes in this book will cover everything from the basics to some surprising creative twists on classics. That said, all will take a seasonal approach because everything (no matter how you cook it) tastes best when in season or feels seasonally appropriate. Just think: Lemony spring vegetable risottos call to mind the freshness of the season, while earthy beef stews warm the winter soul. One-pot cooking will free up your time and energy so you can actually enjoy and savor that time of year, both in and out of the kitchen. While some seasonal ingredients can be found and enjoyed year-round—such as hothouse tomatoes—it's good to know when they're naturally in season, since that's when they taste their best.

SPRING

- Artichokes
- Arugula
- Asparagus
- Lamb
- Peas
- Rhubarb
- Spinach
- Strawberries

SUMMER

- Basil
- Berries
- Cherries
- Crab
- Eggplant
- Figs
- Green beans
- Melons
- Peaches
- Peppers
- Stone fruit
- Summer squash
- Tomatoes
- Watermelon

FALL

- Apples
- Fennel

- Kale
- Pumpkin

WINTER

- Brussels sprouts
- Citrus
- Greens (kale, collards, chard)

- Pomegranates
- Root vegetables
- Winter squash

Recipe Labels

In the recipes ahead, you'll notice labels that give you a quick snapshot when you need to consider things like allergies and time.

Dairy-Free: These recipes have no milk or any ingredients that come from cow's milk (cheese, sour cream, cottage cheese, etc.).

Gluten-Free: These recipes do not include gluten, a protein found in grains such as wheat, barley, and rye.

Vegetarian: These recipes have no meat (beef, chicken, pork, etc.) in them, including meat byproducts.

Nut-Free: These recipes do not contain nuts of any kind or nut oils.

Worth the Wait: You've all heard the old adage that "good food takes time." It's never more true than when you sit down to a slow-cooked meal. While most dishes will be ready to eat in less than 45 minutes, I've included a few that take longer, but it's usually due to hands-off time spent in the oven. Definitely worth the wait!

Tips

At the bottom of each recipe, you'll find little tips to guide you along the way.

Helpful Hint: Trust us, these little tips will make your cooking so much easier and quicker!

Variation: Cooking is often about personal preference and expression. While we'll show you the traditional way to prepare the dish, there are always variations in methods and ingredients that you might want to explore.

In Season Now: We'll point out what's in peak season so you can incorporate it into your dish to create unbelievable flavor.

Alt Pot: Just because we recommend a particular piece of cookware in a recipe doesn't mean it's the only thing you can or should use. Give an alternative pot a try and see what happens.

SPRING

Now is the season for tender asparagus and gorgeous strawberries ripe off the vine, tangy goat cheese, and even lamb. The frost of Old Man Winter has blown away, making room for the warm colors of emerging blossoms and delicate baby greens. In this way, each meal becomes a celebration of all that nature offers—both on the plate and on the other side of your front door.

Green Hominy Soup

SERVES 6 | PREP TIME: 15 MIN | COOK TIME: 3 TO 8 HOURS

DAIRY-FREE / GLUTEN-FREE / NUT-FREE / WORTH THE WAIT

Often referred to as pozole in Spanish, hominy is a dried corn that has been soaked in an alkaline solution to increase its nutritional value. The solution is rinsed off, and the result is a delicious ingredient that thickens this light soup and can also be used to make tortillas.

1. In a slow cooker, combine the olive oil, pork chops, onion, garlic, chili powder, cumin, chipotle, cayenne, chicken stock, and green chiles and season with salt and pepper. Cook on high for 2 to 3 hours or on low for 5 to 7 hours.

2. Add the hominy and cook for 1 more hour, until the pork is tender.

3. Serve in bowls garnished with lime wedges and cilantro.

VARIATION Pork is traditionally used in pozole, but chicken would be equally as delicious.

2 tablespoons extra-virgin olive oil

1 pound boneless pork chops, thinly sliced

1 onion, diced

3 garlic cloves, minced

1 tablespoon chili powder

1 teaspoon ground cumin

1 chipotle pepper (canned in adobo), chopped

⅛ teaspoon cayenne pepper

3 cups low-sodium chicken stock

1 (4-ounce) can chopped green chiles

Salt and black pepper

1 (15-ounce) can hominy

1 lime, cut into wedges

2 tablespoons chopped fresh cilantro

Italian Bean Soup

SERVES 4 | PREP TIME: 15 MIN | COOK TIME: 45 MIN

DAIRY-FREE / VEGETARIAN / NUT-FREE

This easy Italian Bean Soup is also known as ribollita, *which means "reboiled"—probably because it improves in flavor when reheated and served the next day as leftovers. It's hearty and satisfying on a chilly spring evening.*

1. In a Dutch oven over medium-high heat the olive oil and sauté the onion, carrot, and celery until softened, 10 to 12 minutes. Add the garlic and cook for 30 seconds.

2. Add the diced tomatoes, beans, bay leaves, thyme, and oregano and season with salt and pepper. Stir well. Bring to a boil and cook for 3 minutes. Lower the heat to medium and simmer for 15 minutes.

3. Add the bread and the kale and cook for 15 minutes more. If the soup becomes too dry, add a bit of water. Season with additional salt and pepper to taste, remove the bay leaves, and serve.

HELPFUL HINT If you decide to use fresh herbs in place of the dried, keep in mind that you will need to use three times as much to get the same flavor. For the freshest flavor, add them just before you serve the soup.

2 tablespoons extra-virgin olive oil

1 onion, diced

1 carrot, peeled and diced

1 celery stalk, diced

3 garlic cloves, minced

1 (14.5-ounce) can diced tomatoes, undrained

1 (15-ounce) can cannellini beans

2 bay leaves

1 teaspoon dried thyme

1 teaspoon dried oregano

Salt and black pepper

2 cups stale whole-wheat bread, cut or torn into bite-size pieces

3 cups chopped baby kale

Chicken Tortilla Soup

SERVES 4 | PREP TIME: 15 MIN | COOK TIME: 35 MIN

DAIRY-FREE / GLUTEN-FREE / NUT-FREE

This soup is bursting with flavor—from the warmth of the seared chicken and fire-roasted tomatoes to the sweetness of the corn. It's everything you love in one bowl.

1. Place the chicken breasts in a freezer bag and pound until about ½ inch thick. Season the chicken breasts with salt, pepper, cumin, and the lime zest.

2. In a stockpot over medium-high heat the olive oil and sauté the chicken breasts until browned on both sides, 8 to 10 minutes. Remove them to a plate and set aside.

3. Add the onion to the pot and sauté until softened, 3 to 4 minutes. Add the garlic and jalapeño and cook for 30 seconds. Add the chicken stock, tomatoes, black beans, corn, lime juice, and browned chicken. Bring to a boil and let cook, stirring, for 3 minutes. Lower the heat to medium, cover, and cook for 15 minutes.

4. Using two forks, shred the chicken and return it to the soup. Add the cilantro and season with additional salt and pepper to taste.

HELPFUL HINT Classic toppings for this soup include tortilla strips, diced avocado, and shredded Monterey Jack cheese. To pick the perfect avocado, you might have to gently squeeze a few. If it doesn't give a bit when you pick it up, it won't be ready to eat that night.

2 skinless, boneless chicken breasts

Salt and black pepper

1 teaspoon ground cumin

Zest and juice of 1 lime, divided

2 tablespoons extra-virgin olive oil

1 onion, diced

3 garlic cloves, minced

1 jalapeño, diced

6 cups low-sodium chicken stock

1 (14.5-ounce) can fire-roasted diced tomatoes

1 (14.5-ounce) can black beans, drained and rinsed

1 (14.5-ounce) can corn, drained

¼ cup chopped fresh cilantro

Mexican Beef Stew

SERVES 4 | PREP TIME: 10 MIN | COOK TIME: 35 MIN

DAIRY-FREE / NUT-FREE

This traditional Mexican beef stew, often referred to as carne guisada, *is perfect served with leftover rice or simply inside warmed tortillas. Feel free to garnish with a bit of sour cream, avocado, and cilantro.*

1. In a large bowl, toss the meat with the flour and season with salt and pepper.

2. Preheat the pressure cooker on sauté and pour in the oil. Brown the beef in batches, 4 to 5 minutes each. Be careful not to overcrowd the pot.

3. Add the onion and cook until softened, 3 to 4 minutes. Add the garlic, jalapeño, beef stock, tomato paste, cumin, and chili and chipotle powders and stir to combine.

4. Close and lock the lid, closing off the vent, and pressure cook on high for 20 minutes. Either allow the pressure cooker to depressurize naturally or carefully slide open the quick release valve.

ALT POT This Mexican beef stew can be prepared in a Dutch oven. Simply brown the beef over medium-high heat in step 2, then follow the next step. To cook the dish, cover the Dutch oven and bake in a 350°F oven for 1½ to 2 hours, or until the beef is fork-tender.

1¾ pounds chuck roast, trimmed and cut into bite-size pieces

3 tablespoons all-purpose flour

Salt and black pepper

2 tablespoons extra-virgin olive oil

1 large onion, diced

4 garlic cloves, minced

2 jalapeño peppers, seeded and minced

2 cups beef stock

2 tablespoons tomato paste

1 tablespoon ground cumin

1 teaspoon chili powder

½ teaspoon chipotle powder

Vegetable Panini

SERVES 4 | PREP TIME: 10 MIN | COOK TIME: 15 MIN

VEGETARIAN / NUT-FREE

Take your favorite sautéed vegetables, layer them between two thick slices of sourdough bread, toast them in butter, and you'll have an incredibly delicious sandwich. Go ahead—eat two. You know you want to.

2 tablespoons extra-virgin olive oil

8 ounces mushrooms, sliced

1 red onion, sliced

1 green bell pepper, thinly sliced

4 garlic cloves, minced

¼ cup sun-dried tomatoes, drained if packed in oil

1 teaspoon dried oregano

1 cup shredded mozzarella cheese

Salt and black pepper

1 (5.2-ounce) package gournay cheese, such as Boursin

8 slices sourdough bread

2 tablespoons butter

1. In a sauté pan over medium-high heat, warm the olive oil. Add the mushrooms, onion, and bell pepper and cook until softened slightly, 5 to 7 minutes. Add the garlic, sun-dried tomatoes, and oregano and cook for 30 seconds. Transfer the mixture to a bowl, add the mozzarella cheese, and toss to combine. Season with salt and pepper to taste.

2. Spread the gournay cheese on each slice of bread. Divide the vegetable mixture on top of four slices. Top with the remaining slices of bread.

3. In the sauté pan over medium heat, melt the butter. Add the sandwiches, cover, and cook until browned, 3 to 4 minutes. Flip and cook, covered, until browned, 3 to 4 minutes. Cut the sandwiches in half and serve.

IN SEASON NOW Mushrooms abound in spring, so this is a great time to try a variety of types. Morels are particularly good. They look like an oblong bulb with goosebumps on the outside. They are rare, but you'll find them each spring for a very short period of time.

Pork Bahn Mi

SERVES 6 | PREP TIME: 15 MIN | COOK TIME: 3 TO 6 HOURS AND 10 MIN

DAIRY-FREE / NUT-FREE / WORTH THE WAIT

This Vietnamese sandwich is the perfect combination of sweet and spicy, hot and cold, crunchy and delicious. Be sure to toast the bun before you assemble the sandwich for extra crunch. Substitute chicken for the pork if you like.

1. Place the pork tenderloin in the slow cooker with ¼ cup rice wine vinegar. Season with salt and pepper. Cook on high for 3 hours or on low for 6 hours. Remove the loin from the slow cooker and let it rest for 10 minutes. Cut it into ½-inch-thick slices.

2. Preheat the oven to 350°F.

3. In a bowl, whisk together the remaining ¼ cup rice wine vinegar and the sugar, until dissolved. Add the cucumber, carrot, daikon, jalapeño, and cilantro and toss to coat.

4. Warm the baguettes in the oven. Split them open and slather one side of each with a little mayonnaise, hoisin sauce, and sriracha. Top with the sliced pork and pickled vegetables.

IN SEASON NOW Many of the vegetables in this dish are available all year round, but spring is truly when radishes are at their peak.

1½ pounds pork tenderloin

½ cup rice wine vinegar, divided

Salt and black pepper

1 tablespoon sugar

1 cucumber, thinly sliced

1 carrot, shredded

1 daikon radish, shredded

1 jalapeño, seeded and minced

¼ cup chopped fresh cilantro

3 baguettes

¼ cup mayonnaise

1 teaspoon hoisin sauce

1 teaspoon sriracha

Spicy Chicken Lettuce Wraps

SERVES 4 | PREP TIME: 15 MIN | COOK TIME: 10 MIN

DAIRY-FREE / NUT-FREE

Looking to reduce your carbs? Give these Spicy Chicken Lettuce Wraps a try and you'll forget you ever wanted bread or rice. Serve with a variety of garnishes, such as thinly sliced carrots, red bell peppers, jalapeños, bean sprouts, crushed peanuts, sweet chili sauce, or peanut sauce.

1. In a bowl, mix together 4 tablespoons brown sugar, 4 tablespoons soy sauce, and 3 teaspoons rice wine vinegar, ⅛ teaspoon sesame oil, the garlic, and 1 teaspoon ground ginger, as well as the spicy mustard, sriracha, cornstarch, and water. Set aside.

2. In a Dutch oven over medium-high, heat the vegetable oil and sauté the onion until translucent, 3 to 4 minutes. Add the ground chicken, remaining 1 teaspoon ginger, and season with salt and pepper. Cook, breaking it up with a wooden spoon.

3. Add the remaining 2 tablespoons brown sugar, 2 tablespoons soy sauce, and ½ teaspoon rice wine vinegar and cook until the chicken is no longer pink. Add the brown sugar mixture from step 1 and simmer until the sauce is thickened slightly, 3 to 4 minutes.

4. Serve in lettuce leaves.

HELPFUL HINT If the sauce does not thicken enough, whisk together 1 tablespoon cornstarch with an equal amount of water and pour it into the pan. Bring to a boil and it will thicken.

6 tablespoons brown sugar, divided

6 tablespoons low-sodium soy sauce, divided

3½ teaspoons rice wine vinegar, divided

¼ teaspoon sesame oil, divided

2 garlic cloves, minced

2 teaspoons ground ginger, divided

1½ tablespoons spicy mustard

1 to 2 teaspoons sriracha

1 teaspoon cornstarch

2 tablespoons water

3 tablespoons vegetable oil

3 tablespoons diced onion

1½ pounds ground chicken

Salt and black pepper

1 head lettuce (Boston, red, or green leaf)

Tequila-Lime Shrimp Tacos

SERVES 4 | PREP TIME: 10 MIN | COOK TIME: 5 MIN

DAIRY-FREE / GLUTEN-FREE / NUT-FREE

This dish is so quick it actually takes less time to cook than it does to prep. If you prefer not to use the tequila, simply omit it, although I think it adds an extra dimension of flavor. These are especially good garnished with cilantro, sour cream, and salsa.

1. In a bowl, toss the shrimp with ½ cup olive oil, the tequila, garlic, coriander, chipotle, lime zest, and salt and pepper.

2. In a sauté pan over medium-high, heat the remaining olive oil and cook the shrimp until browned on both sides, 3 to 4 minutes.

3. Serve in warmed corn tortillas and garnish with the cilantro.

HELPFUL HINT My favorite way to warm up corn tortillas is to hold them over an open gas flame on a gas stovetop, just until they are nicely browned around the edges. Be careful not to leave them unattended, or they'll go up in flames quickly!

1 pound shrimp (size 21/25), peeled and deveined

⅔ cup extra-virgin olive oil, divided

¼ cup tequila

4 garlic cloves, minced

2 teaspoons ground coriander

½ teaspoon chipotle powder

2 teaspoons grated lime zest

Salt and black pepper

6 corn tortillas

¼ cup chopped fresh cilantro

Poblano Poppers

SERVES 4 | PREP TIME: 10 MIN | COOK TIME: 35 MIN

GLUTEN-FREE / VEGETARIAN / NUT-FREE

If you like the idea of jalapeño poppers, but not the heat, give this recipe a chance. Poblanos are a milder pepper that pairs well with this smoky savory stuffing. Have plenty of sour cream, guacamole, and sliced jalapeños on hand to finish off this dish.

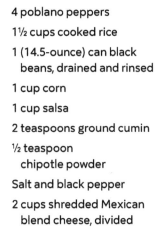

4 poblano peppers

1½ cups cooked rice

1 (14.5-ounce) can black beans, drained and rinsed

1 cup corn

1 cup salsa

2 teaspoons ground cumin

½ teaspoon chipotle powder

Salt and black pepper

2 cups shredded Mexican blend cheese, divided

1. Set an oven rack six inches below the broiler and preheat the broiler. Cut the poblano peppers in half lengthwise. Place them in a 9-by-13-inch baking dish and broil them until they blister and blacken, 6 to 8 minutes per side. Place the peppers in a plastic freezer bag, seal, and let steam for 5 minutes. Carefully remove the skin from the peppers and return them to the baking dish.

2. Preheat the oven to 350°F. In a large bowl, mix together the rice, beans, corn, salsa, cumin, chipotle powder, salt, pepper, and 1 cup shredded cheese.

3. Fill each of the peppers with the rice mixture. Top with the remaining cheese. Bake for 15 minutes and serve hot.

HELPFUL HINT While you can eat the skin on the peppers, it's so much nicer if you take it off, and the easiest way is to let steam do the work for you. If you don't want to use your broiler, you can hold the peppers (with long tongs) over an open gas burner on your stovetop.

Falafel

SERVES 4 | PREP TIME: 1 HOUR 20 MIN | COOK TIME: 16 MIN

DAIRY-FREE / VEGETARIAN / NUT-FREE / WORTH THE WAIT

Falafel, made with chickpeas and a variety of herbs and spices, are so delicious and versatile. Serve them atop a salad or nestled in a warm pita. Pair them with plenty of tzatziki sauce and your favorite hummus on the side to round out the meal.

1. Line a sheet pan with parchment paper.

2. In a food processor, combine the chickpeas, parsley, cilantro, onion, flour, lemon juice, baking powder, cumin, cayenne, salt, pepper, and garlic. Pulse until well blended and uniform in size.

3. Scoop out 2 tablespoons of dough and, with wet hands, form it into a ball and place it on the prepared sheet pan. Repeat with the rest of the mixture. You will have about 12 balls. Place another sheet of parchment on top of the balls and press down gently to form them into disks. Place the tray in the refrigerator to chill for 1 hour.

4. Preheat the oven to 400°F. Meanwhile, remove the falafel from the fridge and discard the parchment paper. Drizzle the vegetable oil over the falafel on the sheet pan. Bake for 8 minutes, flip, and bake for 8 minutes more. Transfer to a paper towel to drain.

1 (15-ounce) can chickpeas, drained and rinsed

1 cup chopped fresh parsley

1 cup chopped fresh cilantro

½ onion, chopped

¼ cup all-purpose flour

2 teaspoons lemon juice

1 teaspoon baking powder

1½ teaspoons ground cumin

½ teaspoon cayenne pepper

1 teaspoon salt

1 teaspoon black pepper

4 garlic cloves

¼ cup vegetable oil

HELPFUL HINT An hour to let the falafel rest can seem like forever, but trust me—if you skip this step, you'll have a big mess. Without the proper time to chill, the dough will dissolve in the hot oven.

Roasted Vegetable Panzanella

SERVES 4 | PREP TIME: 15 MIN | COOK TIME: 20 MIN

VEGETARIAN / NUT-FREE

The classic Italian salad is simply toasted bread and tomatoes with a bit of basil and Parmesan. This version makes a full meal out of it by adding roasted bell peppers, squash, and eggplant, making it even more colorful than the traditional recipe.

1. Preheat the oven to 400°F and place a sheet pan inside.

2. Once the oven comes to temperature, place the bread cubes on the sheet pan and toss with 3 tablespoons olive oil and the garlic, salt, and pepper. Bake for 8 minutes or until the bread is toasted. Remove from the pan and set aside.

3. In a large bowl, toss the bell pepper, squash, eggplant, and onion with 2 tablespoons olive oil plus additional salt and pepper. Spread out on the sheet pan and roast for 10 minutes, or until they are softened. Add the cherry tomatoes and basil, stirring well to combine.

4. In a measuring cup, whisk together the balsamic vinegar, honey, and remaining 4 tablespoons olive oil. Season with salt and pepper to taste.

5. In a serving bowl, combine the croutons with the roasted vegetables. Dress with the vinaigrette and garnish with Parmesan.

IN SEASON NOW If squash isn't your favorite vegetable, consider using asparagus, fennel, or leeks, which are also in season.

10 ounces whole-grain bread, cut into 1-inch cubes

9 tablespoons extra-virgin olive oil, divided

4 garlic cloves, minced

Salt and black pepper

1 red bell pepper, diced

1 yellow squash, diced

1 eggplant, diced

½ red onion, sliced

1 pound cherry tomatoes, halved

¼ cup fresh basil, torn

¼ cup balsamic vinegar

2 tablespoons honey

¼ cup shaved Parmigiano-Reggiano

Niçoise Salad

SERVES 4 | PREP TIME: 20 MIN | COOK TIME: 30 MIN

DAIRY-FREE / GLUTEN-FREE / NUT-FREE

A stockpot is exactly what you'll need for this classic dish from France. The components can be made well in advance and arranged on the plate when you're ready to serve.

1. Place the eggs in a stockpot with enough water to cover them by 1 inch and bring to a boil. Turn off the heat and let the eggs sit in the hot water for 11 minutes. Remove the eggs with a slotted spoon, reserving the water in the pot, and place them in an ice bath. Once the eggs are cool enough to handle, peel and cut them in half.

2. Heat the water to boiling again and add the green beans to the stockpot. Cook until crisp-tender, 3 minutes. Remove the beans, reserving the water, and place them in the ice bath to stop the cooking. Drain.

3. Put the potatoes in the stockpot and cook until fork-tender, 8 minutes.

4. Place the lettuce on a serving plate. Arrange the other ingredients in groups on top of the lettuce: eggs, green beans, potatoes, tomatoes, shallot, olives, and tuna.

5. In a small bowl, whisk together the white wine vinegar, olive oil, mustard, and honey. Season with salt and pepper to taste. Drizzle the dressing over the salad.

HELPFUL HINT Be sure to plunge your green beans into ice water after they have cooked. Not only will this prevent them from overcooking, but it will also preserve their beautiful bright green color.

4 large eggs

Ice for an ice bath

½ pound green beans

½ pound baby or fingerling potatoes, quartered

1 head Boston bibb lettuce

8 cherry tomatoes, halved

1 shallot, diced

½ cup Niçoise olives, pitted

2 (5.5-ounce) cans tuna packed in oil, drained

¼ cup white wine vinegar

½ cup extra-virgin olive oil

1 teaspoon Dijon mustard

2 teaspoons honey

Salt and black pepper

Mushroom, Spinach, and Artichoke Penne

SERVES 4 | PREP TIME: 15 MIN | COOK TIME: 25 MIN

VEGETARIAN / NUT-FREE

In the mood for a creamy, cheesy vegetarian treat? This pasta dish is just what you're craving, and it's filled with springtime spinach to welcome the season. The red pepper flakes give it a bit of spice, though you can omit them if you don't like spicy food.

1. Bring a stockpot of salted water to a boil over high heat. Cook the penne until al dente, 12 to 14 minutes. Drain in a colander and set aside.

2. In the same stockpot, melt the butter over medium-high heat, then sauté the onion, mushrooms, and artichoke hearts until the onion is softened, 3 to 4 minutes.

3. Add the spinach and garlic and cook, stirring, until the spinach is wilted. Season with salt, pepper, and red pepper flakes.

4. Add the half-and-half and Parmesan and bring to a boil. Cook until it thickens slightly, about 5 minutes. Add the pasta back to the pot and stir to combine.

5. Add the basil and season with additional salt and pepper to taste.

VARIATION You can use any kind of pasta, but it's best with a variety that has some shape to it (shells, macaroni, rigatoni) so the delicious sauce has something to cling to.

8 ounces penne

2 tablespoons butter

½ onion, diced

4 ounces cremini mushrooms, thinly sliced

1 (14-ounce) can artichoke hearts, drained, quartered

2 cups chopped fresh spinach

2 garlic cloves, minced

Salt and black pepper

¼ teaspoon red pepper flakes

1 cup half-and-half

1 cup grated Parmigiano-Reggiano

¼ cup chopped fresh basil

Veggie Lo Mein

SERVES 4 | PREP TIME: 15 MIN | COOK TIME: 15 MIN

DAIRY-FREE / VEGETARIAN / NUT-FREE

Who needs takeout when you have this recipe on hand? In mere minutes dinner is on the table, loaded with beautiful fresh vegetables, including spinach, mushrooms, carrot, red bell pepper, and snow peas. Grab a box of fortune cookies to get the full experience.

1. Fill a stockpot two-thirds full with water, bring to a boil over high heat, and cook the lo mein noodles until they are al dente, about 3 minutes. Drain in a colander and set aside.

2. In the stockpot over medium-high heat the oil and sauté the carrot, bell pepper, and snow peas until softened, 6 to 8 minutes. Add the mushrooms, garlic, and spinach and cook until softened, 2 to 3 minutes.

3. In a small bowl, whisk together the soy sauce, sugar, sesame oil, ginger, and sriracha.

4. Return the noodles to the stockpot with the vegetables. Add the soy sauce mixture, tossing well to coat. Season with salt and pepper to taste.

IN SEASON NOW This recipe is really just a guideline—use whatever vegetables are in season and what you prefer.

8 ounces lo mein noodles

1 tablespoon extra-virgin olive oil

1 carrot, thinly sliced

1 red bell pepper, thinly sliced

2 ounces (½ cup) snow peas

2 cups sliced mushrooms

2 garlic cloves, minced

3 cups chopped fresh spinach

2 tablespoons low-sodium soy sauce

2 teaspoons sugar

1 teaspoon sesame oil

½ teaspoon grated fresh ginger

½ teaspoon sriracha

Salt and black pepper

Pasta Puttanesca

SERVES 4 | PREP TIME: 10 MIN | COOK TIME: 35 MIN

DAIRY-FREE / NUT-FREE

This infamous dish is often referred to by the unfortunate name of "whore's sauce," as it was a pantry-friendly meal that Italian ladies of the evening could throw together after an exhausting night at work. It's incredibly easy and delicious, whatever you call it.

1. Fill a stockpot two-thirds full with water, bring to a boil over high heat, and cook the pasta until al dente, about 14 minutes. Drain in a colander and set aside in a serving bowl.

2. In the stockpot, heat the oil over medium-high heat and sauté the garlic and anchovies until the anchovies dissolve. Be careful not to burn the garlic.

3. Lower the heat to medium, add the tomatoes and red pepper flakes, and cook for 10 minutes. If the sauce is too thick, add some of the reserved tomato juice.

4. Add the capers and olives, season with salt and pepper to taste, and simmer for another 10 minutes. Serve over the penne.

HELPFUL HINT This dish scares some people because of the anchovies. Fear not! They don't taste fishy at all in this dish. Instead, they bring a savory umami flavor that is out of this world.

1 pound penne

3 tablespoons extra-virgin olive oil

3 garlic cloves, minced

6 anchovy fillets or 2 tablespoons anchovy paste

1 (28-ounce) can crushed tomatoes, drained, juice reserved

1 teaspoon red pepper flakes

3 tablespoons capers, drained and rinsed

1 cup oil-cured olives

Salt and black pepper

Cauliflower and Bacon Gratin

SERVES 4 | PREP TIME: 15 MIN | COOK TIME: 45 MIN

NUT-FREE

We've all heard the saying, "everything's better with bacon." But if you prefer to go vegetarian, leave it out and use butter or olive oil in its place.

1. Preheat the oven to 350°F.

2. In a skillet over high heat, bring the cauliflower and water to a boil. Cover and cook for 6 minutes, or until tender. Drain and set aside.

3. Reduce the heat to medium, add the bacon and cook until crispy, 8 to 10 minutes. Drain on a paper towel. Pour off any excess fat from the skillet, leaving 2 tablespoons in the pan and 1 in a small bowl. Crumble the bacon.

4. Heat the pan again over medium heat and whisk the flour into the fat, stirring for 2 minutes. Slowly pour in the milk, whisking constantly, and cook until the milk thickens, 4 to 5 minutes. Reduce the heat to low and whisk in the mustard, Gruyère, ¼ cup Parmesan, and nutmeg. Season with salt and pepper.

5. Add the cauliflower and bacon back into the skillet, tossing to coat with the sauce.

6. In the bowl, toss the bread crumbs with the remaining ¼ cup Parmesan and 1 tablespoon bacon grease. Spread over the cauliflower.

7. Bake for 20 minutes, until the top is nicely browned.

VARIATION Not a huge fan of cauliflower? Vegetable gratins can be made with any vegetable you prefer. Broccoli would be a great substitution.

1 head cauliflower, cut into florets

½ cup water

4 slices bacon

3 tablespoons all-purpose flour

2 cups milk

2 teaspoons Dijon mustard

1 cup grated Gruyère

½ cup grated Parmigiano-Reggiano, divided

¼ teaspoon ground nutmeg

Salt and black pepper

⅓ cup bread crumbs

Quesadilla Pie

SERVES 4 | PREP TIME: 15 MIN | COOK TIME: 1 HOUR

NUT-FREE

Expect people to go back for seconds after they get a taste of these layers of spicy meat and tons of gooey cheese. Serve with avocado, salsa, and sour cream.

1. Preheat the oven to 350°F.

2. In a 10-inch oven-safe skillet over medium-high heat, brown the ground beef until fully cooked, 6 to 8 minutes. Drain off any excess fat, leaving 1 to 2 tablespoons in the pan.

3. Add the onion and sauté until softened, 3 to 4 minutes. Add the garlic and cook for 30 seconds. Add the black beans, tomatoes, cumin, cayenne, and cooked beef, mixing well. Season with salt and pepper to taste. Transfer to a bowl.

4. Place one tortilla on the bottom of the skillet. Top with one-third of the filling. Sprinkle on about one-third of the shredded cheese. Repeat with the rest of the tortillas, filling, and cheese, finishing with one last flour tortilla with a little cheese on top.

5. Cover the skillet with aluminum foil and bake for 30 minutes. Remove the foil and cook for another 10 minutes, until the top is lightly browned. Let cool for 10 minutes before cutting into quarters and serving.

VARIATION Ground beef is the traditional protein for this dish, but you can substitute ground chicken, turkey, sausage, or plant-based meats. Or you can forgo them altogether and have a fabulous vegetarian meal.

1 pound lean ground beef

1 onion, diced

4 garlic cloves, minced

1 (14.5-ounce) can black beans, drained and rinsed

2 (14.5-ounce) cans diced fire-roasted tomatoes

2 teaspoons ground cumin

½ teaspoon cayenne pepper

Salt and pepper

4 large flour tortillas

1 pound shredded Mexican blend cheese

Poached Eggs in Spicy Tomato Sauce

SERVES 4 | PREP TIME: 10 MIN | COOK TIME: 10 MIN

GLUTEN-FREE / VEGETARIAN / NUT-FREE

Also known as shakshuka, this traditional Middle Eastern dish is simply a spicy tomato sauce that acts as a nest for poached eggs. This is one of those dishes that is usually served for breakfast, but it works just as well for lunch or dinner. Serve it with flatbread to soak up the savory sauce.

1. In a 10-inch sauté pan over medium-high heat the olive oil and sauté the onion and bell pepper until they soften, 3 to 4 minutes.

2. Add the garlic and cook for 30 seconds. Add the tomatoes, paprika, cumin, cayenne, and salt and pepper, mixing well. Lower the heat to medium and simmer.

3. Create a little well in the tomatoes for each of the four eggs. Crack the eggs into a small bowl and place one in each well. Season the eggs with additional salt and pepper, cover, and cook just until the eggs set up, 3 to 4 minutes. You want the yolks to be runny.

4. Serve garnished with lemon juice, feta, and cilantro.

HELPFUL HINT It's important you don't overcook the eggs. If the yolks cook too much, you won't have the beautiful sauce they create as you cut into them.

2 tablespoons extra-virgin olive oil

1 onion, diced

1 red bell pepper, diced

3 garlic cloves, minced

1 (28-ounce) can diced tomatoes

2 teaspoons smoked paprika

1 teaspoon ground cumin

½ teaspoon cayenne pepper

Salt and black pepper

4 large eggs

Juice of ½ lemon

¼ cup crumbled feta

3 tablespoons chopped fresh cilantro

Teriyaki Salmon with Asparagus

SERVES 4 | PREP TIME: 5 MIN | COOK TIME: 15 MIN

DAIRY-FREE / NUT-FREE

Not only is this dish gorgeous and packed full of good-for-you antioxidants, it is one of the easiest meals you'll ever make. That makes it ideal for putting together on a busy weeknight when you'd like to eat a nutritious meal but didn't think you had the time. Besides, who doesn't love the combination of teriyaki, salmon, and asparagus? This is great over leftover rice or grains.

1. Preheat the oven to 400°F. Line a sheet pan with parchment paper.

2. Place the salmon fillets on one side of the sheet pan and the asparagus on the other side.

3. Drizzle the asparagus with the olive oil. Season everything with salt and pepper. Roast for 8 minutes.

4. Brush the salmon with the teriyaki sauce and bake for 4 more minutes.

5. Garnish with sesame seeds and serve.

4 (6-ounce) salmon fillets

1 pound asparagus, trimmed

1 tablespoon extra-virgin olive oil

Salt and black pepper

1 cup teriyaki sauce

2 teaspoons sesame seeds

IN SEASON NOW Not a huge fan of asparagus? Spring is full of produce. Try substituting snow peas, sugar snap peas, or zucchini.

Roasted Salmon with Potatoes and Fennel

SERVES 4 | PREP TIME: 12 MIN | COOK TIME: 35 MIN

DAIRY-FREE / GLUTEN-FREE / NUT-FREE

Be sure the potatoes are more than halfway cooked before you place the salmon on top. If not, you'll end up with crunchy potatoes and overcooked fish. If that happens, pop the potatoes and fennel back into the oven for a few extra minutes before topping them with the fish.

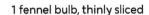

1. Preheat the oven to 375°F.

2. In a 9-by-13-inch baking dish, toss the fennel, potatoes, and garlic with 2 tablespoons olive oil and salt and pepper. Roast for 20 minutes.

3. Place the salmon fillets and tomatoes on top of the fennel and potatoes. Drizzle with the remaining 2 tablespoons olive oil and season with additional salt and pepper. Roast for 15 minutes.

4. Drizzle with lemon juice and serve.

IN SEASON NOW Spring is when fennel is at its best. If you don't love its bold licorice flavor raw, try it roasted, which mellows it. It's delicious.

1 fennel bulb, thinly sliced

1 pound baby fingerling potatoes, quartered

4 garlic cloves, minced

4 tablespoons extra-virgin olive oil, divided

Salt and black pepper

6 (6-ounce) salmon fillets

1 cup halved grape tomatoes

2 tablespoons lemon juice

Potato-Crusted Salmon with Garlic Green Beans

SERVES 4 | PREP TIME: 12 MIN | COOK TIME: 35 MIN

GLUTEN-FREE / NUT-FREE

Salmon is wonderful on its own, but when you form a crust on it with seasoned shredded potatoes, it is transformed into something magical. Plus, it's all cooked en papillote, *a classic French method for steaming it in paper (or in our case, aluminum foil), which makes the cleanup super-quick and easy.*

1. Preheat the oven to 450°F.

2. Arrange four 10-by-10-inch square pieces of aluminum foil on a work surface and liberally coat them with the butter. Place a piece of salmon on each piece of foil and season lightly with salt and pepper.

3. In a bowl, mix together the shredded potatoes, lemon juice, and scallions and season with additional salt and pepper. Arrange the potatoes around the salmon. Tightly wrap each package and place in a 9-by-13-inch baking dish. Bake for 15 minutes.

4. Move the foil packages to one side of the baking dish and place the green beans on the other side. Drizzle the green beans with the olive oil and sprinkle on the garlic and additional salt and pepper. Bake for an additional 10 minutes.

2 tablespoons butter

4 (6-ounce) salmon fillets

Salt and black pepper

2 potatoes, shredded

2 tablespoons lemon juice

2 scallions, chopped

½ pound green beans

1½ tablespoons extra-virgin olive oil

3 garlic cloves, minced

5. Transfer the green beans to a plate, cover, and set aside to keep warm. Set the oven to broil and place the rack 2 to 3 inches below the broiler element.

6. Carefully open the foil packets, leaving them in the baking dish. Broil for 4 to 6 minutes, or until the potatoes are slightly browned. Serve warm with the green beans.

VARIATION This dish is so versatile. Substitute any fish or vegetable you prefer. Remember that thinner fish will cook more quickly and denser vegetables will take longer, so adjust the cook times as needed.

Shrimp Risotto

SERVES 4 | PREP TIME: 12 MIN | COOK TIME: 40 MIN

GLUTEN-FREE / NUT-FREE

This dish is one that demands your undivided attention, but it is oh-so-worth-it when you take that first bite of creamy, cheesy Arborio rice.

1. Season the shrimp with the salt and pepper. In a sauté pan over medium-high heat, melt 2 tablespoons butter and sear the shrimp until just cooked, 2 to 3 minutes. Transfer the shrimp to a plate and cover to keep warm.

2. Add the shallot and the remaining 1 tablespoon butter to the pan and sauté until softened, 3 to 4 minutes. Add the garlic and cook for 30 seconds. Add the wine and cook, stirring to deglaze the pan, until it has nearly evaporated. Add the rice and stir until fully coated.

3. Microwave the chicken stock for 5 minutes, until hot. Gradually add ½ cup stock to the sauté pan, whisking constantly. Cook until nearly all of the stock has been absorbed by the rice, then add another ½ cup stock. Continue to do this until the rice is cooked and al dente, 20 to 25 minutes.

4. Stir in the cheese and season to taste with additional salt and pepper. Remove to a serving bowl, top with the shrimp, and garnish with the parsley.

1 pound shrimp (size 21/25), peeled and deveined

Salt and black pepper

3 tablespoons butter, divided

1 shallot, diced

2 garlic cloves, minced

½ cup dry white wine

1 cup Arborio rice

2½ cups low-sodium chicken stock

½ cup grated Parmigiano-Reggiano

2 tablespoons chopped fresh parsley

IN SEASON NOW Risotto is often served with spring peas. Not only do they make a pretty addition to the dish, they also add a pop of texture.

Asparagus and Shrimp Stir-Fry

SERVES 4 | PREP TIME: 10 MIN | COOK TIME: 10 MIN

DAIRY-FREE / NUT-FREE

Stir-fries are perfect for those nights you need to eat fast. This recipe is no exception—dinner will be on the table in less than 15 minutes, and you'll be rewarded with an amazing meal made with fresh ingredients. Try serving this over leftover cooked rice.

1. In a sauté pan over high heat the oil and cook the asparagus and mushrooms until softened, 4 to 6 minutes.

2. Add the shrimp, garlic, and ginger and cook until the shrimp are pink, 1 to 2 minutes.

3. In a measuring cup, combine the chicken stock, soy sauce, and cornstarch, whisking until smooth. Pour into the skillet, stir, bring to a boil, and cook until thickened, about 1 minute. Season with salt and pepper to taste.

IN SEASON NOW If you really want to up the vegetable count in this dish, don't limit yourself to asparagus. Throw in a variety of colors—I suggest carrots and bell peppers of every color.

2 tablespoons extra-virgin olive oil

1 pound asparagus, trimmed, cut into thirds

8 ounces cremini mushrooms, quartered

¾ pound shrimp (size 21/25), peeled and deveined

4 garlic cloves, minced

1 (½-inch) piece ginger, peeled and grated

½ cup low-sodium chicken or vegetable stock

¼ cup low-sodium soy sauce

1 tablespoon cornstarch

Salt and black pepper

Teriyaki Chicken with Pineapple Rice

SERVES 4 | PREP TIME: 15 MIN | COOK TIME: 35 MIN

DAIRY-FREE / NUT-FREE

Can't make it to Hawaii except in your dreams? This dish will get you into the spirit of the tropics. If you prefer this recipe a little sweeter, use some of the pineapple juice in place of the chicken stock.

1. In a measuring cup, whisk together the soy sauce, vinegar, sriracha, sesame oil, garlic, and ginger to make a teriyaki sauce.

2. Season the chicken with salt and pepper. Then, in a 12-inch sauté pan over medium-high heat the olive oil and sear the chicken until browned, 10 to 12 minutes per side. Transfer the chicken to a plate.

3. Add the rice to the pan, stirring to coat with any remaining oil. Add the chicken stock and crushed pineapple, stir, bring to a boil, and cook for 2 minutes.

4. Reduce the heat to medium-low and nestle the chicken and broccoli florets on top of the rice. Drizzle with the teriyaki sauce. Cover and cook until the chicken reaches a temperature of 165°F, an additional 8 minutes.

HELPFUL HINT Getting a nice sear on the chicken and cooking it more at the beginning of the recipe is the key to having it finish at the same time as the rice in one skillet.

½ cup low-sodium soy sauce

¼ cup apple cider vinegar

1½ teaspoons sriracha

1 teaspoon sesame oil

2 garlic cloves, minced

1 teaspoon minced ginger

4 skinless, boneless chicken breasts or thighs

Salt and black pepper

2 tablespoons vegetable oil

1½ cups rice (such as Uncle Ben's converted)

3 cups low-sodium chicken stock

1 cup crushed pineapple, drained

2 cups broccoli florets

Spanish Chicken and Rice

SERVES 4 | PREP TIME: 10 MIN | COOK TIME: 1 HOUR 10 MIN

DAIRY-FREE / GLUTEN-FREE / NUT-FREE / WORTH
THE WAIT

Also known as arroz con pollo *(rice with chicken),*
this classic dish is a filling combination of seared
chicken, creamy rice, and, in this variation, green
olives. The comfort-food flavors of this recipe make
it a big winner for both young and old.

1. Preheat the oven to 350°F.

2. Season the chicken with the smoked paprika
   and salt and pepper. In a Dutch oven over
   medium heat the oil and brown the chicken,
   skin-side down for 10 to 12 minutes. Flip the
   chicken and cook until browned on the opposite side, another 10 to 12 minutes. Transfer the
   chicken to a plate.

3. Add the onion and sauté until softened, 3 to
   4 minutes. Add the garlic and cook for another
   30 seconds. Add the wine and cook, stirring
   to deglaze the pan, until the liquid is nearly
   evaporated.

4. Add the rice, chicken stock, tomatoes, and saffron, mixing well. Nestle the chicken on top of
   the rice and top with the olives. Cover and bake
   in the oven for 30 minutes, or until all of the
   liquid has been absorbed.

HELPFUL HINT Don't want to spend the money for saffron?
You can get the same yellow coloring effect with ½ teaspoon
ground turmeric for a fraction of the price.

4 skin-on, bone-in
chicken thighs

1 tablespoon
smoked paprika

Salt and black pepper

2 tablespoons extra-virgin
olive oil

1 onion, diced

4 garlic cloves, minced

⅓ cup dry white wine

1 cup white rice

2 cups low-sodium
chicken stock

1 cup diced tomatoes

Pinch saffron

¾ cup green olives

Asian Sheet-Pan Chicken

SERVES 4 | PREP TIME: 12 MIN | COOK TIME: 45 MIN

DAIRY-FREE / NUT-FREE

Feeling extra spicy? Add as much sriracha as you like to kick up the heat in this one-dish dinner. Plus, making dinner on a sheet pan is about the easiest thing in the world. By using bone-in chicken thighs, the meat stays tender and juicy.

1. Preheat the oven to 375°F. Line a sheet pan with parchment paper.

2. In a small bowl, combine the hoisin, soy sauce, sriracha, vinegar, sesame oil, and garlic.

3. Place the onion, bell pepper, and chicken on the sheet pan and season with salt and pepper. Add half the hoisin mixture and toss to combine. Roast for 30 minutes.

4. Add the snow peas and toss with the ingredients on the pan. Roast for another 10 to 12 minutes, or until the chicken is cooked through and reaches an internal temperature of 165°F.

5. Top with the remaining hoisin mixture and return to the oven for 2 minutes. Serve garnished with bean sprouts.

HELPFUL HINT Hoisin sauce is really just an Asian barbecue sauce. If it's not in your store, try making your own with a combination of your favorite barbecue sauce and a touch of molasses and soy sauce.

¼ cup hoisin sauce

⅓ cup low-sodium soy sauce

2 tablespoons sriracha, plus more for garnish

2 teaspoons rice wine vinegar

2 teaspoons sesame oil

4 garlic cloves, minced

1 onion, cut into 1-inch pieces

1 red bell pepper, cut into 1-inch pieces

4 skin-on, bone-in chicken thighs

Salt and black pepper

4 ounces (1 cup) snow peas

1 cup bean sprouts

Lemon and Rosemary Roasted Chicken

SERVES 6 | PREP TIME: 10 MIN | COOK TIME: 35 MIN

DAIRY-FREE / GLUTEN-FREE / NUT-FREE

The heady aroma of chicken roasting in the oven is intoxicating enough, but add in rosemary and lemon and you have something really special. Any leftover chicken can be shredded and used in tacos or salads.

1. Preheat the oven to 375°F.

2. Place the chicken, potatoes, and carrots in a 9-by-13-inch baking dish. Drizzle with the olive oil and lemon juice and add the garlic. Season with salt and pepper. Top with the rosemary sprigs.

3. Roast for 30 to 35 minutes, or until the chicken reaches an internal temperature of 165°F.

HELPFUL HINT If the idea of cutting up a whole chicken scares you (and you're not alone), grab a package of precut chicken or ask your butcher to do it for you.

1 (3- to 5-pound) chicken, cut into 8 pieces

½ pound baby potatoes

½ pound baby carrots

3 tablespoons extra-virgin olive oil

Juice of 1 lemon

4 garlic cloves, minced

Salt and black pepper

4 sprigs rosemary

Cashew Chicken

SERVES 4 | PREP TIME: 15 MIN | COOK TIME: 2 TO 3 HOURS

DAIRY-FREE / WORTH THE WAIT

Want to have Chinese takeout waiting for you when you get home? Pop everything into the slow cooker, go out and run some errands or have fun with your family, and when you return, dinner is served.

1. In a slow cooker, mix together the chicken, bell pepper, onion, broccoli, soy sauce, vinegar, honey, garlic, ginger, and red pepper flakes.

2. Cook on low for 2 to 3 hours. Season with salt and pepper to taste and garnish with cashews and scallions.

HELPFUL HINT Not all soy sauce is gluten-free. Be sure to read the labels and choose wisely.

3 skinless, boneless chicken breasts, cut into bite-size pieces

2 red bell peppers, diced

1 onion, diced

1 head broccoli, cut into florets

¼ cup low-sodium soy sauce

¼ cup rice wine vinegar

3 tablespoons honey

4 garlic cloves, minced

1 (2-inch) piece ginger, peeled and grated

½ teaspoon red pepper flakes

Salt and black pepper

¾ cup unsalted cashews

2 scallions, chopped

Penne with Sun-Dried Tomatoes and Chicken

SERVES 4 | PREP TIME: 15 MIN | COOK TIME: 30 MIN

NUT-FREE

Sun-dried tomatoes were all the rage back in the 80s, and they still deserve a place at the table. Their concentrated flavor brings a real intensity to the dish. Be sure to hydrate them well and cut them into small pieces before serving or they can be a bit chewy. Serve with a side salad and garlic bread.

1. Fill a sauté pan two-thirds full with salted water and bring to a boil over high heat. Add the pasta and cook until al dente, about 14 minutes. Drain in a colander and set aside.

2. In the same sauté pan over medium-high heat the olive oil and cook the chicken until cooked through, 6 to 8 minutes.

3. Add the shallot and cook until it's translucent, 3 to 4 minutes. Add the sun-dried tomatoes and cook for 2 minutes. Stir in the heavy cream and cook for 2 more minutes.

4. Add in the butter, Parmesan, and basil and stir to combine. Season with salt and pepper to taste and serve over the hot penne.

VARIATION Want to go gluten-free with this dish? Gluten-free pastas work just as well. Consult the package for directions on the proper cook time.

½ pound penne

1 tablespoon extra-virgin olive oil

2 skinless, boneless chicken breasts, cut into 1-inch pieces

1 shallot, finely diced

8 ounces sun-dried tomatoes, drained if in oil, chopped

1 cup heavy cream

1 tablespoon butter

⅓ cup grated Parmigiano-Reggiano

⅓ cup chopped fresh basil

Salt and black pepper

Garlic-Parmesan Chicken

SERVES 4 | PREP TIME: 10 MIN | COOK TIME: 50 MIN

GLUTEN-FREE / NUT-FREE

Put your pressure cooker to good use by making this garlicky chicken, cream, spinach, and cheese dish that results in a deliciously simple weeknight meal. The lemon juice brightens the flavors and will lure you back to make it again.

1. Season the chicken with salt, pepper, and Italian seasoning.

2. Preheat the pressure cooker on sauté. Add the olive oil and chicken to brown, 8 to 10 minutes per side. You will need to do this in two batches.

3. Return all of the chicken to the pot, then add in the heavy cream, garlic, and Parmesan. Close and lock the lid, closing off the vent, and pressure cook on high for 15 minutes. Either allow the pressure cooker to depressurize naturally or carefully slide the quick release button. Open the pot and add the spinach and lemon juice. Close the lid and let sit until the spinach wilts, about 5 minutes.

4. If the sauce is too thin for your taste, remove the chicken from the pot and cover it to stay warm. Turn the pressure cooker to sauté and let the liquid to cook down until it thickens, 5 to 6 minutes. Season with additional salt and pepper to taste and serve over the chicken.

ALT POT This simple dish can easily be made in a Dutch oven, sauté pan, or skillet. Brown the chicken, make the sauce, and nestle the chicken back in the sauce to finish cooking, 8 to 10 minutes.

4 skinless, boneless chicken breasts

Salt and black pepper

1 tablespoon Italian seasoning

2 tablespoons extra-virgin olive oil

1 cup heavy cream

4 garlic cloves, minced

½ cup grated Parmigiano-Reggiano

3 cups chopped fresh spinach

2 tablespoons lemon juice

Chicken Cacciatore

SERVES 6 | PREP TIME: 10 MIN | COOK TIME: 3 TO 8 HOURS

DAIRY-FREE / GLUTEN-FREE / NUT-FREE / WORTH THE WAIT

This pantry-friendly dinner makes use of ingredients you probably already have. It's great any night of the week, but I think it's even better for a lazy Sunday supper. This dish is traditionally served over egg noodles, but is satisfying all on its own.

1. In a slow cooker, mix together the chicken, onion, bell pepper, mushrooms, tomatoes, garlic, red wine, Italian seasoning, and red pepper flakes and season with salt and pepper.

2. Cover and cook on low for 6 to 8 hours, or on high for 3 to 4 hours, until the chicken is cooked throughout.

ALT POT This dish is also fabulous prepared in a Dutch oven or an electric pressure cooker. Season and sear the chicken until golden brown and add the remaining ingredients. In a Dutch oven, cover and cook for about 1 hour in a 350°F oven; in a pressure cooker, cook for about 20 minutes on high.

6 skinless, bone-in chicken thighs

1 onion, diced

1 green bell pepper, diced

8 ounces mushrooms, quartered

1 (28-ounce) can whole tomatoes

4 garlic cloves, minced

¼ cup dry red wine

1 tablespoon Italian seasoning

1 teaspoon red pepper flakes

Salt and black pepper

Three-Cheese Alfredo with Sausage and Shrimp

SERVES 4 | PREP TIME: 15 MIN | COOK TIME: 20 MIN

NUT-FREE

Pasta with cream sauce is a fan favorite, but you can take it to the next level with the addition of sautéed shrimp and sausage. Have your significant other bring home a loaf of garlic bread, and dinner is served.

1. Fill a Dutch oven two-thirds full with salted water and bring to a boil over high heat. Add the linguine and cook until al dente, 9 minutes. Drain, cover, and set aside.

2. Heat the same Dutch oven over medium-high heat and brown the sausage all over, adding olive oil if necessary.

3. Add the shrimp and cook until pink, 2 to 3 minutes. Add the garlic and cook for 30 seconds. Add the wine and cook, stirring to deglaze the pan.

4. Add the heavy cream, chicken stock, and chipotle peppers and bring to a boil. Cook until slightly thickened.

5. Reduce the heat to medium and whisk in the fontina, Parmesan, and mozzarella. Add the cooked linguine and toss to coat. Season with salt and pepper. Garnish with parsley and serve.

HELPFUL HINT This dish combines three cheeses. Use any three you prefer, but keep in mind you want at least one that brings creaminess and melts well (such as fontina or mozzarella) and one that has great nuttiness and depth of flavor (such as Parmesan).

1 pound linguine

½ pound Italian sausage

1 tablespoon extra-virgin olive oil (if needed)

½ pound shrimp (size 21/25), peeled and deveined

3 garlic cloves, minced

⅓ cup dry white wine

1 cup heavy cream

1 cup low-sodium chicken stock

1 teaspoon chipotle peppers in adobo sauce, minced

1 cup shredded fontina

½ cup shredded Parmigiano-Reggiano

¼ cup shredded mozzarella

Salt and black pepper

1 tablespoon minced fresh parsley

Honey-Orange Roasted Lamb Chops

SERVES 4 | PREP TIME: 10 MIN | COOK TIME: 10 MIN

DAIRY-FREE / GLUTEN-FREE / NUT-FREE

Spring lamb is one of nature's great treats. This dish is light and succulent with its combination of freshly squeezed orange juice, honey, and mint.

1. Preheat the oven to 400°F. Line a sheet pan with parchment paper.

2. In a measuring cup, combine the orange juice, honey, mint, vinegar, cumin, and mustard and season with salt and pepper.

3. Place the lamb chops on the sheet pan and rub the spice mixture evenly over the chops. Add the asparagus to the pan.

4. Roast for 4 minutes. Flip the chops and roast for 4 more minutes. Garnish with orange zest and serve with the juices from the pan.

VARIATION If you don't love lamb, this seasoning combination works equally well with pork.

¼ cup freshly squeezed orange juice

1 tablespoon honey

¼ cup chopped fresh mint

1 tablespoon balsamic vinegar

2 teaspoons ground cumin

1 teaspoon dry mustard

Salt and black pepper

8 (4-ounce) lamb chops

1 pound asparagus, trimmed

1 tablespoon orange zest

Ham and Cheese Bread Pudding

SERVES 4 | PREP TIME: 10 MIN | COOK TIME: 40 MIN

NUT-FREE

While this dish was designed for dinner, no one is stopping you from serving it as an easy, hearty breakfast or crowd-friendly brunch entrée. It reheats well and makes a filling lunch for the next day as well.

1. Preheat the oven to 400°F.

2. Place the cubed bread in an 8-by-8-inch baking dish and bake the bread until toasted, about 8 minutes.

3. Add the onion, garlic, ham, spinach, Gruyère, and mozzarella to the baking dish and stir to combine. Season with salt and pepper.

4. In a measuring cup, combine the milk and eggs and pour it over the bread mixture, making sure to cover all the bread.

5. Bake for 30 minutes, or until browned.

HELPFUL HINT Don't skip toasting the bread. It really helps to keep it from getting too soggy after you add the other ingredients.

4 cups cubed whole-grain bread or sourdough

1 small onion, diced

3 garlic cloves, minced

4 ounces smoked ham, diced

8 ounces frozen spinach, thawed, drained

1 cup grated Gruyère

½ cup shredded mozzarella

Salt and black pepper

1 cup milk

3 large eggs

Spicy Pork Ramen

SERVES 4 | PREP TIME: 15 MIN | COOK TIME: 12 MIN

DAIRY-FREE / NUT-FREE

Ramen is all your favorite things in one spicy bowl: succulent pork and lots of noodles in an aromatic broth. And the best part? This one comes together in mere minutes, which is a blessing when you have hungry, impatient children.

1. In a stockpot over high heat, mix together the chicken stock, ginger, garlic, red pepper flakes, and pork and bring to a boil. Reduce the heat to medium and simmer until the pork is cooked, 6 to 7 minutes. The pork can be slightly pink.

2. Add the noodles, mushrooms, and bok choy and cook until the noodles are cooked, about 4 minutes.

3. Add the soy sauce and sesame oil and garnish with the scallions. Serve hot.

VARIATION If you can't find baby bok choy (or even regular bok choy), feel free to substitute spinach or Asian cabbage.

4 cups low-sodium chicken stock

1 tablespoon grated ginger

4 garlic cloves, minced

½ teaspoon red pepper flakes

1 pound pork tenderloin, cut into 3-by-½-inch strips

2 (3-ounce) packages dried ramen noodles

4 ounces shiitake mushrooms, sliced

1 bunch baby bok choy, chopped

2 teaspoons low-sodium soy sauce

1 teaspoon sesame oil

2 scallions, chopped

Jamaican Jerk Pork

SERVES 4 | PREP TIME: 5 MIN | COOK TIME: 40 MIN

DAIRY-FREE / GLUTEN-FREE / NUT-FREE

Now you can have slow-roasted, pull-apart jerk pork in a fraction of the time with the help of your pressure cooker. It's delicious served with a side of rice and beans or in a sandwich, though you may find yourself sneaking pieces every time you pass the refrigerator.

1. Preheat the pressure cooker to sauté. Rub the pork with the jerk spice blend.

2. Add the pork to the pot and cook in the olive oil until browned, turning the pork to brown it all sides.

3. Add the pineapple juice. Close and lock the lid, closing off the vent, and pressure cook on high for 30 minutes. Either allow the pressure cooker to depressurize naturally or carefully slide the quick release button.

4. Using two forks, shred the pork and place it on a plate. Top the pork with the sauce from the pot.

ALT POT This dish can also be made in a Dutch oven. Brown the pork, cover, and roast in a 350°F oven for 1 hour 30 minutes, or until the meat is tender and shreds easily.

2 pounds pork shoulder

¼ cup Jamaican jerk spice blend

1 tablespoon extra-virgin olive oil

¼ cup pineapple juice

Sausages with Bell Peppers, Onions, and Baby Potatoes

SERVES 4 | PREP TIME: 10 MIN | COOK TIME: 20 MIN

DAIRY-FREE / GLUTEN-FREE / NUT-FREE

This is a meal all on its own, but it also makes delicious sandwiches. In that case, consider skipping the potatoes or serve them on the side. You could save the potatoes and make home-fried potatoes another time.

1. Preheat the oven to 400°F. Line a sheet pan with parchment paper.

2. Place the sausages, red and green bell pepper, onion, and potatoes on the sheet pan and toss with the tomatoes, garlic, oregano, and red pepper flakes. Season with salt and pepper.

3. Roast for 20 minutes or until the sausages are cooked through.

HELPFUL HINT It's a good idea to slightly prick each one of your sausages with the tip of a sharp paring knife so they don't burst while cooking.

4 bratwurst or Italian sausages

1 red bell pepper, cut into long slices

1 green bell pepper, cut into long slices

1 onion, cut into slices

½ pound baby potatoes, halved

1 (15-ounce) can crushed tomatoes

3 garlic cloves, chopped

2 teaspoons dried oregano

½ teaspoon red pepper flakes

Salt and black pepper

Paella

SERVES 4 | PREP TIME: 20 MIN | COOK TIME: 25 MIN

DAIRY-FREE / GLUTEN-FREE / NUT-FREE

Full of succulent seafood, sausage, rice, and toma-toes, this dish is meant for a crowd. Spanish chorizo differs from Mexican chorizo in that it is already fully cooked and can be eaten right out of the pack-age. Mexican chorizo (which you could also use) must be cooked before consuming.

1. In a bowl, add the saffron to the fish stock and stir to dissolve. Set aside.

2. In a 12-inch sauté pan over medium-high heat the oil and sauté the shrimp until pink, 1 to 2 minutes. Transfer the shrimp to a plate and set aside.

3. In the same pan, sauté the onion until softened, 4 to 5 minutes. Add the garlic and cook for 30 seconds.

4. Raise the heat to high, add tomatoes, and cook until the liquid from the tomatoes almost com-pletely evaporates.

5. Add the rice and sauté for 1 minute. Add the mussels, fish stock, clam juice, chorizo, and smoked paprika and cook for 5 minutes.

6. Lower the heat to medium and cook another 7 minutes.

7. Add the shrimp and peas and cook for 3 minutes. Serve hot.

IN SEASON NOW The peas might seem like an afterthought, but they bring the fresh brightness of spring to this dish.

¼ teaspoon saffron

2 cups fish or low-sodium chicken stock

2 tablespoons extra-virgin olive oil

½ pound shrimp (size 21/25), peeled and deveined

1 onion, diced

4 garlic cloves, minced

1 (14.5-ounce) can whole tomatoes, broken up

1½ cups short grain rice

10 mussels

1 cup clam juice

4 Spanish chorizo, diced

½ teaspoon smoked paprika

½ cup peas

Indian-Spiced Meatballs in Curry Sauce

SERVES 4 | PREP TIME: 12 MIN | COOK TIME: 30 MIN

GLUTEN-FREE / NUT-FREE

These meatballs are delicious, but make sure to have a spoon handy because you are going to want to eat the sauce all by itself. Serve it over basmati rice or with plenty of warm naan.

1. In a large bowl, mix together the lamb, grated ginger, 2 tablespoons curry powder, cayenne, and yogurt and season with salt and pepper.

2. Using a cookie scoop, form golf ball–size meatballs. In a sauté pan over medium-high heat the olive oil, add the meatballs, and cook until browned but not cooked through, 8 to 10 minutes. Transfer to a plate.

3. Pour out any excess fat, leaving 1 tablespoon in the pan. Add the onion and cook until softened, 3 to 4 minutes. Add the garlic and remaining ginger and cook for 30 seconds.

4. Add the curry paste, tomatoes, half-and-half, and remaining ½ tablespoon curry powder and whisk to combine. Return the meatballs to the pan, toss to coat with the sauce, bring to a boil, and cook for 2 minutes. Reduce the heat to medium-low, cover and simmer for 15 minutes. Garnish with cilantro and serve.

VARIATION If you don't like lamb, you can always use ground beef, pork, or chicken in this dish.

1 pound ground lamb

1 (2-inch) piece ginger, half grated and the other half left whole

2½ tablespoons curry powder, divided

¼ teaspoon cayenne pepper

2 tablespoons plain yogurt

Salt and black pepper

1 tablespoon extra-virgin olive oil

1 large onion, chopped

3 garlic cloves, minced

3 tablespoons Indian curry paste

1 (14.5-ounce) can diced tomatoes

½ cup half-and-half

¼ cup chopped fresh cilantro

Braised Lamb with Fennel and Orange

SERVES 4 | PREP TIME: 15 MIN | COOK TIME: 30 MIN

DAIRY-FREE / GLUTEN-FREE / NUT-FREE

The sweet smell of lamb mingles with the fennel and orange in this dish to create the perfect spring dinner.

1. Preheat the pressure cooker on sauté and pour in the olive oil. Season the lamb with salt and pepper, add it to the pot, and brown for 5 to 6 minutes. Transfer to a plate.

2. Add the fennel and onion to the pot and sauté until softened, 4 to 5 minutes. Add the garlic and cook for 30 seconds. Add the wine and stir to deglaze the pan. Turn off sauté mode.

3. Add the bay leaves, cinnamon stick, tomatoes, and lamb. Close and lock the lid, closing off the vent, and pressure cook on high for 15 minutes. Either allow the pressure cooker to depressurize naturally or carefully slide the quick release button.

4. Season with salt and pepper and drizzle with honey and balsamic vinegar. Remove the bay leaves and garnish with orange zest.

ALT POT Don't have an electric pressure cooker? This dish comes together beautifully in a Dutch oven as well. Plan on cooking it in a 350°F oven for about 1 hour 30 minutes.

2 tablespoons extra-virgin olive oil

2 pounds lamb shoulder

Salt and black pepper

1 fennel bulb, chopped

1 onion, diced

6 garlic cloves, minced

1 cup dry white wine

2 bay leaves

1 cinnamon stick

1 (14.5-ounce) can diced tomatoes

2 tablespoons honey

2 tablespoons dark balsamic vinegar

Zest of 1 orange

Stuffed Bell Peppers

SERVES 4 | PREP TIME: 15 MIN | COOK TIME: 30 MIN

GLUTEN-FREE / NUT-FREE

The filling for this recipe, with spicy sausage, mushrooms, and marinara, goes well with the green bell peppers and is topped off with luscious melty cheese. Try making these with red or yellow bell peppers for a milder flavor.

1. Preheat the oven to 350°F.

2. Fill a Dutch oven two-thirds full with water and bring to a boil over high heat. Add the bell peppers and blanch in the boiling water until tender, about 5 minutes. Drain and set aside.

3. Reheat the Dutch oven over medium-high heat, add the oil, sausage, and onion, and sauté until the sausage is thoroughly cooked and the onion is softened, 5 to 6 minutes. Add the mushrooms and cook until softened, 3 to 4 minutes. Add the garlic and cook for 30 seconds.

4. Add the marinara sauce, half of the mozzarella, and the Parmesan cheese and stir to combine.

5. Fill each bell pepper with the sausage mixture and stand them upright in the Dutch oven. Top with the remaining mozzarella cheese and bake for 15 minutes. Serve hot.

HELPFUL HINT If your bell peppers don't want to stand up on their own, cut a little off the bottom. Just be careful not to cut completely through the pepper so the filling won't leak out.

4 green bell peppers, tops cut off and seeds removed

1 tablespoon extra-virgin olive oil

1 pound spicy Italian sausage

1 onion, diced

8 ounces button mushrooms, quartered

4 garlic cloves, minced

2 cups marinara sauce

1½ cups shredded mozzarella, divided

½ cup grated Parmigianno-Reggiano

Salt and black pepper

Steak Fajitas

SERVES 6 | PREP TIME: 15 MIN | COOK TIME: 10 MIN

DAIRY-FREE / NUT-FREE

Fajitas are typically grilled, but this indoor, roasted version works in any season or any night of the week. Serve with plenty of salsa, sour cream, and guacamole. A squeeze of lime juice is nice to give it a little added pop.

1. Preheat the oven to 400°F. Line a sheet pan with parchment paper.

2. Place the steak, bell peppers, onion, and garlic on the sheet pan and toss with the olive oil.

3. In a small bowl, combine the cumin, chili powder, onion powder, and red pepper flakes and season with salt and pepper. Sprinkle the mixture over the steak and vegetables and toss to combine.

4. Roast for 10 minutes. Serve with warmed tortillas.

VARIATION Flank or skirt steak are traditionally used when making fajitas. They are incredibly flavorful, but can be a little tough, which is why I always cut them against the grain to tenderize them.

2 pounds flank or skirt steak, thinly sliced against the grain

1 red bell pepper, cut into slices

1 yellow bell pepper, cut into slices

1 green bell pepper, cut into slices

2 onions, thinly sliced

6 garlic cloves, minced

2 tablespoons extra-virgin olive oil

2 teaspoons ground cumin

2 teaspoons chili powder

1 teaspoon onion powder

1 teaspoon red pepper flakes

Salt and black pepper

6 to 8 (10-inch) flour tortillas

Szechuan Beef with Snow Peas

SERVES 4 | PREP TIME: 12 MIN | COOK TIME: 5 MIN

DAIRY-FREE / NUT-FREE

Red pepper flakes are the source of the spice in this recipe, so feel free to add more or use less to make it as spicy as you like. You could also add chopped asparagus, which is a nice spring vegetable.

1. In a measuring cup, combine the soy sauce, sherry, brown sugar, cornstarch, garlic, ginger, and red pepper flakes.

2. In a sauté pan over medium-high heat, add the oil, steak, and snow peas and cook until the steak is browned, 2 to 3 minutes. Add the sauce, bring to a boil, and cook until it thickens, about 1 minute. Season with salt and pepper to taste and serve.

HELPFUL HINT When seasoning dishes that have soy sauce in them (even low-sodium soy), be careful not to add as much salt as you normally would, otherwise your meal can get way too salty.

⅓ cup low-sodium soy sauce

2 tablespoons dry sherry

1 tablespoon brown sugar

1 tablespoon cornstarch

4 garlic cloves, minced

2 teaspoons grated ginger

1 teaspoon red pepper flakes

1½ tablespoons vegetable oil

1 pound flank or skirt steak, thinly sliced against the grain

6 ounces (1½ cups) snow peas

Salt and black pepper

Slow-Cooked Cuban Beef

SERVES 6 | PREP TIME: 10 MIN | COOK TIME: 4 TO 8 HOURS

DAIRY-FREE / GLUTEN-FREE / NUT-FREE /
WORTH THE WAIT

This succulent slow-cooked Cuban beef dish, often referred to as ropa vieja, *is made by cooking a chuck roast for hours until it becomes so tender it resembles tattered or "old clothes"—hence the name in Spanish. It's delicious served with rice and beans.*

1. Put the roast, onion, bell pepper, garlic, wine, paprika, oregano, tomatoes, bay leaves, olives, vinegar, and sazon in a slow cooker and cook on high 4 hours or on low for 8 hours.

2. Season with salt and pepper to taste, remove the bay leaves, and serve.

HELPFUL HINT Sazon seasoning is a type of seasoned salt found in Spanish and Mexican markets. To make your own, mix together 1 tablespoon each ground coriander, cumin, turmeric, and garlic powder plus 2 teaspoons dried oregano, 1 teaspoon onion powder, and 1 teaspoon salt. It can be stored in a sealed container at room temperature for about 6 months.

1 (3- to 4-pound)
   chuck roast, cut into
   1-inch cubes
2 onions, diced
2 red bell peppers, diced
8 garlic cloves, minced
¼ cup dry white wine
1 tablespoon paprika
1 tablespoon
   dried oregano
1 (28-ounce) can diced
   tomatoes
2 bay leaves
¾ cup green olives
1 tablespoon white vinegar
1 packet sazon seasoning
Salt and black pepper

SUMMER

To celebrate the wonderful vegetables that are so abundant in the summer months, start by buying whatever has just been harvested at your local farmers' market or roadside produce stand. Whatever you can't find there can be purchased at a regular grocery store. Look for tomatoes, corn, mixed greens, and fresh herbs like basil and cilantro that are at their very best this time of year. Warmer weather also means not spending a lot of time in a hot kitchen, so this is a great time to use your electric pressure cooker or slow cooker, spend your days outside, and come home to dinner.

Fruit Risotto

SERVES 4 | PREP TIME: 10 MIN | COOK TIME: 15 MIN

GLUTEN-FREE / VEGETARIAN / NUT-FREE

Sometimes you just want a warm breakfast in the morning—or something a little sweet for dinner. The aroma of spiced apples, brown sugar, and butter is just the thing to get everyone excited.

1. Preheat the pressure cooker on sauté. Add the apples, 2 tablespoons butter, and ½ teaspoon cinnamon and sauté until the apples are soft, 4 to 5 minutes. Transfer the mixture to a plate and set aside.

2. Add the rice and the remaining 1 tablespoon butter to the pot and stir to coat. Add the remaining ½ teaspoon cinnamon, the salt, and nutmeg and stir to combine.

3. Add the apple juice, brown sugar, and vanilla. Close and lock the lid, closing off the vent, and pressure cook on high for 6 minutes. Either allow the pressure cooker to depressurize naturally or carefully slide the quick release button. Serve hot.

ALT POT This breakfast risotto can be made in a Dutch oven or skillet. Follow steps 1 to 2 as instructed. Add the brown sugar and vanilla and stir to incorporate. Gradually add ½ cup apple juice, stirring constantly. As the liquid is absorbed, add another ½ cup until all of the liquid is absorbed and the rice is tender, 20 to 25 minutes.

2 Gala apples, peeled and diced

3 tablespoons butter, divided

1 teaspoon ground cinnamon, divided

1 cup Arborio rice

1 teaspoon salt

¼ teaspoon ground nutmeg

4 cups apple juice

¼ cup packed brown sugar

¾ teaspoon vanilla extract

Tomato-Basil Soup

SERVES 4 | PREP TIME: 5 MIN | COOK TIME: 25 MIN

DAIRY-FREE / GLUTEN-FREE / VEGETARIAN / NUT-FREE

You will never want canned soup again after you make this incredibly quick and easy version. It's very good on its own, but croutons or shredded Cheddar cheese make a nice addition.

1 tablespoon extra-virgin olive oil

3 garlic cloves, minced

1 (28-ounce) can diced tomatoes

3 cups low-sodium vegetable broth

Salt and black pepper

¼ cup thinly sliced fresh basil, divided

1. In a Dutch oven over medium heat the olive oil and sauté the garlic for 30 seconds, stirring constantly. Stir in the tomatoes and cook for 2 minutes. Add the broth, stir, and bring to a boil. Reduce the heat to medium-low and simmer for 20 minutes. Season with salt and pepper to taste. Stir in the basil, reserving 1 tablespoon for garnish.

2. Using an immersion blender, puree the soup until smooth. Garnish with the reserved basil and serve.

IN SEASON NOW Summer is the time for tomatoes, often in overabundance. It's a great time to use them in a recipe like this.

Corn Chowder

SERVES 4 | PREP TIME: 15 MIN | COOK TIME: 2 TO 3 HOURS

GLUTEN-FREE / NUT-FREE / WORTH THE WAIT

Hot soup and summer don't always go together but when you have an abundance of farm-fresh corn, you won't mind one bit. By using a slow cooker, you won't need to hang around in a hot kitchen.

1. In the slow cooker, mix together the onion, corn, thyme, garlic, chicken stock, half-and-half, and potatoes and season with salt and pepper. Cook on high for 2 hours or on low for 3 hours.

2. If you would like to thicken the soup, mash 1 cup of the potatoes and return it to the soup. Garnish with bacon bits and parsley and serve.

IN SEASON NOW Fresh corn is at its peak during the summer months. You don't need to precook it. Just cut the kernels off the cob and add them to the slow cooker.

½ onion, diced

3 cups corn

1 teaspoon dried thyme

4 garlic cloves, minced

4 cups low-sodium chicken stock

2 cups half-and-half

1 pound potatoes, diced

Salt and black pepper

¼ cup bacon bits

1 tablespoon chopped fresh parsley

Thai Shrimp and Coconut Soup

SERVES 4 | PREP TIME: 15 MIN | COOK TIME: 15 MIN

DAIRY-FREE / GLUTEN-FREE / NUT-FREE

This soup sounds like it should be complicated and difficult to make, but nothing is further from the truth. You will be amazed and thrilled at how much flavor you create in such a short amount of time.

1. In a stockpot, over medium heat, add the oil, shallot, garlic, ginger, and chile pepper and sauté for 2 to 3 minutes.

2. Add the chicken stock, coconut milk, lemongrass, and lime zest and bring to a boil. Add the mushrooms and fish sauce and simmer for 10 minutes. Add the shrimp and cook until they turn pink, 2 to 3 more minutes. Stir in the lime juice and season with salt and pepper to taste. Garnish with the cilantro and serve.

HELPFUL HINT Lemongrass looks like a branch of beach grass. It can be very woody, making it difficult to cut. Save yourself the trouble and give it a good smash with the handle of your chef's knife, which will release its great flavor. If you can't find lemongrass, use lemon zest in its place. It won't be quite the same flavor, but it will give you the bright, fresh flavor that's so nice in this dish.

1 tablespoon extra-virgin olive oil

2 shallots, finely diced

3 garlic cloves, minced

1 (1-inch) piece ginger, grated

1 red chile, seeded and finely diced

4½ cups low-sodium chicken stock

1¾ cups unsweetened coconut milk

2 lemongrass stalks, cut into thirds and crushed

Zest and juice of 1 lime

2 cups button mushrooms, sliced

2 tablespoons fish sauce

1 pound shrimp (size 21/25), peeled and deveined

Salt and black pepper

⅓ cup chopped fresh cilantro leaves

Chicken Bruschetta

SERVES 4 | PREP TIME: 15 MIN | COOK TIME: 24 MIN

GLUTEN-FREE / NUT-FREE

Bruschetta is a mouthwatering combination of ripe, luscious tomatoes, garlic, and basil atop grilled bread. In this version we've replaced the bread with seared chicken, but bread would be wonderful to serve with it.

1. In small bowl combine 1 tablespoon olive oil, 6 teaspoons garlic, and the thyme, oregano, and dried basil.

2. Season the chicken with salt and pepper and drizzle with the olive oil–herb mixture.

3. In the small bowl, combine half of the tomatoes, plus the Parmesan, mozzarella, the remaining 2 teaspoons garlic, 1 tablespoon balsamic vinegar, and 2 tablespoons olive oil. Set aside.

4. Add the remaining 1 tablespoon olive oil to the Dutch oven, add the chicken, and cook over medium heat until the chicken is opaque along the top edges, 6 to 8 minutes. Flip each breast and add the fresh basil and the remaining half of the tomatoes, and cook for 4 to 6 minutes.

5. Drizzle with the remaining 1 tablespoon balsamic vinegar and cook until the chicken is no longer pink in the middle, 2 to 4 minutes. Sprinkle with the tomato-cheese mixture and let sit until the cheese melts.

IN SEASON NOW Few raw ingredients are better than an in-season fully ripe tomato. Nothing else will do in this recipe.

4 tablespoons extra-virgin olive oil, divided

8 teaspoons minced garlic, divided

1 teaspoon dried thyme

½ teaspoon dried oregano

½ teaspoon dried basil

4 skinless, boneless chicken breasts, thinly sliced or pounded to ½ inch thick

Salt and black pepper

2 large tomatoes, diced and divided

⅓ cup grated Parmigiano-Reggiano

4 ounces shredded mozzarella

¼ cup chopped fresh basil

2 tablespoons balsamic vinegar, divided

Mahi Mahi Fish Tacos

SERVES 4 | PREP TIME: 10 MIN | COOK TIME: 10 MIN

GLUTEN-FREE / NUT-FREE

More people should really know how absolutely wonderful fish tacos are. This deliciously simple recipe will have you feeling like you're dining by the water in Key West. A cold beer or frozen margarita may be in order.

1. Set an oven rack six inches below the broiler. Preheat the broiler.

2. In a small bowl, combine the oregano, thyme, paprika, and cayenne and season with salt and pepper. Rub each fish fillet with olive oil, then with the seasoning mix. Place the fillets in a 9-by-13-inch baking dish.

3. Broil the fish until firm and cooked through, 6 to 8 minutes.

4. Serve the fish in warmed tortillas topped with cabbage, sour cream, salsa, avocado, and lime wedges, or your favorite toppings.

HELPFUL HINT Broiling is a super-easy way to cook these fillets. Just don't go too far away while they're cooking. The broiler generates very intense heat and can burn the fish before you know it. Don't use parchment paper under these, as it can catch fire under the broiler.

½ teaspoon dried oregano

½ teaspoon dried thyme

¼ teaspoon smoked paprika

⅛ teaspoon cayenne pepper

Salt and black pepper

4 (6-ounce) mahi mahi fillets

1½ tablespoons extra-virgin olive oil

8 flour or corn tortillas

2 cups shredded cabbage

½ cup sour cream

½ cup salsa

2 avocados, pitted and diced

1 lime, cut into wedges

Southwestern Fajitas

SERVES 4 | PREP TIME: 15 MIN | COOK TIME: 10 MIN

DAIRY-FREE / NUT-FREE

If you want your guests to get the full restaurant sizzle when you serve this, bring the skillet screaming hot to the table and let everyone make their own.

1. Season the pork with the cumin, garlic powder, salt, and pepper.

2. In a large skillet over medium-high heat 2 tablespoons olive oil and sear the pork until browned, 3 to 4 minutes. Transfer to a plate and set aside.

3. Add the remaining 1 tablespoon olive oil, onion, and bell peppers and sauté until softened, 3 to 4 minutes.

4. Add the pork back into the sauté pan, stir to combine, and cook until warmed through.

5. Serve the pork and vegetables over warm flour tortillas. Garnish with avocado, cilantro, sour cream, and salsa, if desired.

VARIATION Pork is delicious in these fajitas, but you can substitute beef or chicken if you prefer.

1½ pounds pork tenderloin, cut into 2-inch pieces

2 teaspoons ground cumin

2 teaspoons garlic powder

Salt and black pepper

3 tablespoons extra-virgin olive oil, divided

1 onion, thinly sliced

1 orange bell pepper, thinly sliced

1 yellow bell pepper, thinly sliced

8 (10-inch) flour tortillas

1 avocado, pitted and diced (optional)

¼ cup chopped fresh cilantro (optional)

Sour cream (optional)

Salsa (optional)

Lemongrass-Sausage Lettuce Wraps

SERVES 6 | PREP TIME: 20 MIN | COOK TIME: 20 MIN

DAIRY-FREE / GLUTEN-FREE / NUT-FREE

The combination of lemongrass, lime zest, and cilantro bring a freshness to this dish that is perfect for any summer dinner and pairs nicely with pork. You can make this dish with ground turkey or chicken as well.

1. In large bowl, mix together the ground pork, scallions, lemongrass, ¼ cup cilantro, salt, lime zest, and garlic. Cover and refrigerate to chill.

2. In a measuring cup, whisk together the sweet chili sauce, rice wine vinegar, and sriracha and set aside.

3. Remove the pork mixture from the refrigerator and shape into twelve 2-inch patties.

4. In a large skillet over medium-high heat the coconut oil, add the pork patties, and cook until browned, 3 to 5 minutes per side. Transfer the patties to a paper towel–lined plate.

5. To serve, stack two lettuce leaves on top of one another to form a cup; place 1 to 2 patties in each cup. Garnish with carrot, mint, and the remaining ¼ cup cilantro. Drizzle with the dressing and serve.

HELPFUL HINT Fresh lemongrass can be difficult to find but most groceries now carry the paste in a tube in the produce section. It's much easier to work with and produces a reasonably good facsimile of fresh lemongrass.

1 pound ground pork

⅓ cup sliced scallions

¼ cup chopped lemongrass or lemongrass puree

½ cup chopped fresh cilantro, divided

Salt

1 teaspoon lime zest

3 garlic cloves, minced

¼ cup sweet chili sauce

2 tablespoons rice wine vinegar

1 tablespoon sriracha

1 tablespoon coconut or vegetable oil

1 head Boston lettuce

1 carrot, peeled and shredded

12 fresh mint leaves, chopped

French Dip

SERVES 4 | PREP TIME: 10 MIN | COOK TIME: 3 TO 8 HOURS

DAIRY-FREE / NUT-FREE / WORTH THE WAIT

This is not a first-date sandwich—it's going to be messy but so delicious. Plan ahead and make sure you have plenty of napkins nearby as you dip the sandwich into the savory jus.

1. In a slow cooker, combine the beef stock and Worcestershire sauce. Top with the onion and chuck roast.

2. Season the chuck roast with oregano, garlic powder, salt, and pepper. Cover and cook on high for 3 to 4 hours or on low for 6 to 8 hours, until the beef is so tender it falls apart in shreds.

3. Cut the baguettes in half or thirds depending on the size sandwich you want. Split the cut baguettes horizontally. Top one half of each sandwich with the shredded beef and two slices of provolone. If you would like to melt the cheese, place the sandwiches on a sheet of aluminum foil atop a baking sheet and heat under the broiler for 2 minutes or until the cheese melts.

4. Serve with a small bowl of the juices from the slow cooker to dip the sandwiches.

VARIATION If you don't have a bottle of Worcestershire sauce in the house, you can always substitute soy sauce or even a bit of fish sauce.

½ cup low-sodium beef stock

2 teaspoons Worcestershire sauce

1 onion, thinly sliced

3 pounds boneless beef chuck roast

2 teaspoons dried oregano

2 teaspoons garlic powder

Salt and black pepper

2 baguettes

4 slices provolone

Flat Iron Steak Salad with Cilantro-Lime Dressing

SERVES 4 | PREP TIME: 15 MIN | COOK TIME: 15 MIN

GLUTEN-FREE / NUT-FREE

Grilled steak is delicious all by itself, but when sliced and placed on top of greens and drizzled with this incredibly fresh cilantro-lime dressing, you'll think you're in heaven.

1. Season the steak with salt and pepper. In a sauté pan over high heat 4 tablespoons of the olive oil and sear the steak until browned, 3 to 4 minutes per side. Transfer to a plate and cover lightly to keep warm.

2. In a blender or food processor, combine the cilantro, jalapeño, garlic, lime juice, yogurt, and remaining ¾ cup olive oil and blend until smooth. Season to taste with salt and pepper.

3. Cut the steak against the grain into ¼-inch-thick slices.

4. Place the greens on plates and top with the onion, tomatoes, avocado, steak, and blue cheese. Serve the dressing on the side.

VARIATION Flat iron steak is similar to a skirt or flank steak, just a little thicker. If you can't find it, feel free to substitute skirt, flank, or (if you're feeling generous) a rib eye.

1 pound flat iron steak

Salt and black pepper

1 cup extra-virgin olive oil, divided

1 bunch fresh cilantro

1 jalapeño, cut in half and seeded

3 garlic cloves

3 tablespoons lime juice

½ cup Greek yogurt

4 cups mixed salad greens

½ red onion, thinly sliced

1 cup halved grape tomatoes

1 avocado, pitted and diced

¼ cup crumbled blue cheese

Thai Steak Salad

SERVES 4 | PREP TIME: 15 MIN | COOK TIME: 20 MIN

DAIRY-FREE / GLUTEN-FREE / NUT-FREE

For those hot summer nights when you can't bear to turn on the oven, this will be your new go-to recipe. Packed with flavor and no oven required, the only heat you'll get will be from the chili paste in the sauce.

1. In a measuring cup, whisk together the lime juice, brown sugar, ginger, garlic, fish sauce, and chili paste.

2. Season the steak with salt and pepper. In a sauté pan over medium-high heat the olive oil and sear the steak 6 minutes per side. Remove from the pan, cover loosely with foil, and let sit for 5 minutes before cutting diagonally across the grain into thin slices. Return the steak to the pan and quickly toss with half of the dressing. Set aside.

3. In a mixing bowl, combine the mixed greens, cabbage, carrot, mint, and cilantro and toss with the remaining half of the dressing. Divide the greens among plates and top with slices of beef.

HELPFUL HINT Fish sauce is one of those ingredients that tends to scare people off, but don't let that deter you. Used sparingly, this ingredient really is crucial to adding a much-needed savory, umami flavor to a dish.

⅓ cup lime juice

1½ tablespoons brown sugar

1 tablespoon grated ginger

1 garlic clove, minced

1 tablespoon fish sauce

1 to 2 teaspoons chili paste

1 (1½-pound) flank steak

Salt and black pepper

1½ tablespoons olive oil

4 cups mixed greens

1 cup thinly sliced red cabbage

½ cup thinly sliced carrots

½ cup loosely packed fresh mint leaves

½ cup loosely packed fresh cilantro leaves

Spaghetti with Fresh Corn and Tomatoes

SERVES 4 | PREP TIME: 10 MIN | COOK TIME: 10 MIN

DAIRY-FREE / VEGETARIAN / NUT-FREE

The foundation of this dish is fresh veggies. Find a farm stand, grab a couple ears of corn and some ripe beefsteak tomatoes, and make the freshest-tasting pasta dish you'll ever eat. Sear the corn a bit to add a roasted flavor to the meal.

1. Fill a large stockpot two-thirds full with salted water and bring to a boil. Cook the spaghetti until al dente, 8 to 9 minutes. Drain.

2. Toss the pasta with the olive oil, corn, tomatoes, basil, and chives. Season with salt and pepper to taste and serve warm.

HELPFUL HINT Use a serrated knife to cut tomatoes; the jagged edge of the knife will cut through the skin without bruising the fruit.

1 pound spaghetti

¼ cup extra-virgin olive oil

1½ cups corn

2 cups diced tomatoes

2 tablespoons chopped fresh basil

1 tablespoon chopped fresh chives

Salt and black pepper

Eggplant Parmesan

SERVES 4 | PREP TIME: 25 MIN | COOK TIME: 30 MIN

VEGETARIAN / NUT-FREE

Eggplant Parmesan in one pan? Usually you have to fry it and then layer it in a baking dish. The trick is to use an oven-proof skillet, so you can start on the stovetop and finish baking in the oven—all in one pan.

1. Preheat the oven to 400°F.

2. Place each eggplant slice on paper towels and sprinkle liberally with salt. Let sit for 10 minutes, flip the eggplant, and repeat the process.

3. Place the eggs in a shallow bowl and beat well.

4. On a plate, mix together the panko crumbs, Italian seasoning, and salt and pepper.

5. Blot each piece of eggplant to dry with paper towels. Dip the eggplant slices into the eggs, then into the crumbs, and set aside.

6. In a large oven-safe skillet over medium-high heat the olive oil and brown the eggplant, 1 minute per side. Place the eggplant back onto paper towels to absorb any oil. Let the pan cool slightly and carefully wipe out any oil and dark crumbs.

7. Pour half the marinara sauce into the skillet. Top with a single layer of eggplant. Sprinkle with half of the mozzarella and Parmesan. Repeat with the sauce, remaining eggplant, and cheeses.

1 eggplant, peeled and cut lengthwise into ¼-inch-thick slices

Salt and black pepper

2 large eggs

2 cups panko bread crumbs

2 tablespoons Italian seasoning

3 tablespoons extra-virgin olive oil

2 cups marinara sauce

1½ cups shredded mozzarella

¼ cup grated Parmigiano-Reggiano

2 tablespoons chopped fresh basil

8. Bake for 15 minutes or until the sauce is hot and the cheese has melted.

9. Broil for 3 to 5 minutes to brown the cheese slightly. Garnish with the basil and serve.

IN SEASON NOW Eggplant is delicious if properly prepared, which means peeling it to remove what will become a chewy exterior if cooked. It also means salting it before cooking to extract as much moisture as possible. While this takes some time, the end result will be well worth it.

Garlic and Olive Oil Pasta

SERVES 4 | PREP TIME: 5 MIN | COOK TIME: 12 MIN

DAIRY-FREE / VEGETARIAN / NUT-FREE

Simpler is better I think, particularly when it comes to food. And it doesn't get much simpler than this classic Italian pasta dish of garlic and olive oil, or as the Italians say, aglio e olio. *Just be sure to use the very best extra-virgin olive oil you can find.*

1. Bring a large sauté pan of salted water to a boil over high heat. Cook the spaghetti until al dente, 9 to 10 minutes. Drain.

2. Combine the olive oil, garlic, red pepper flakes, parsley, and lemon zest in the sauté pan, season with salt and pepper, and warm over medium heat for 2 minutes.

3. Add the spaghetti to the pan and toss well before serving.

HELPFUL HINT If you want your salted water to boil faster, use a lid to cover the pot or pan.

1 pound spaghetti

½ cup extra-virgin olive oil

4 garlic cloves, minced

½ teaspoon red pepper flakes

2 tablespoons minced fresh parsley

Zest of 1 lemon

Salt and black pepper

Barbecue Chicken Pizza

SERVES 4 | PREP TIME: 15 MIN | COOK TIME: 35 MIN

NUT-FREE

Almost every grocery store now carries refrigerated pizza dough and, although I make my own when I can, store-bought is very good. It keeps in the refrigerator for a couple of days, or you can freeze it for a month or two. That means pizza night is whenever you say it is.

1. Preheat the oven to 350°F. Line a sheet pan with parchment paper and place it inside the oven.

2. Season the chicken with olive oil, salt, and pepper. Place it on the sheet pan and roast for 20 minutes, or until the chicken is cooked. Let cool slightly and shred.

3. Increase the oven temperature to 450°F.

4. Roll or stretch out the pizza dough to the desired size. Place it on the sheet pan lined with parchment.

5. Top the dough with barbecue sauce, shredded chicken, onion, and cheese. Bake for 12 minutes or until the crust and cheese are lightly browned.

HELPFUL HINT Save yourself a ton of time and hassle shredding the chicken by hand. While it's still hot, put it in your stand mixer bowl fitted with the paddle attachment. It will shred your chicken effortlessly.

2 skinless, boneless chicken breasts

1 tablespoon extra-virgin olive oil

Salt and black pepper

1 refrigerated pizza dough or premade crust

1 cup barbecue sauce

½ red onion, thinly sliced

2 cups shredded Colby or Monterey Jack

Pasta Carbonara

SERVES 4 | PREP TIME: 10 MIN | COOK TIME: 20 MIN

NUT-FREE

Sometimes you just need a big plate of pasta with cream sauce to make it all better. This ultimate one-pot pasta is just the thing, with its combination of bacon and cheese that will improve anyone's day.

1. In a stockpot over medium-high heat, cook the bacon until crispy, 8 to 9 minutes. Transfer to papers towels and let drain. Crumble the bacon and set aside. Wipe out any excess bacon fat from the pot with a paper towel.

2. Fill the stockpot two-thirds full with salted water and bring to a boil. Add the linguini and cook until al dente, 9 to 10 minutes. Drain the pasta and return it to the stockpot.

3. In a measuring cup, whisk together the heavy cream, eggs, garlic, Parmesan, and chipotle pepper. Reduce the heat to low, add the cream mixture to the hot pasta, and toss quickly and thoroughly. If it looks like the egg is beginning to scramble, remove the pot from the heat. Stir until the sauce thickens and coats the pasta. Season to taste with salt and pepper. Divide the pasta among plates and garnish with the crumbled bacon.

4 strips bacon
¾ pound linguine
1 cup heavy cream
4 large eggs
3 garlic cloves, minced
2 cups grated Parmigiano-Reggiano
1 chipotle pepper, minced
Salt and black pepper

HELPFUL HINT Be very careful as you add the egg mixture to the hot pasta to make sure the egg doesn't cook and scramble instead of coating the pasta like a sauce. Start with low or no heat and be prepared to move the pot off the heat entirely if it appears to be cooking the eggs.

Slow-Cooked Pork with "Pancakes"

SERVES 4 | PREP TIME: 15 MIN | COOK TIME: 4 TO 6 HOURS

DAIRY-FREE / NUT-FREE / WORTH THE WAIT

Love moo shu pork, but think it's going to be too difficult to make at home? Try our streamlined, slow-cooker version. While you can always make your own pancakes, it's just as yummy to use flour tortillas.

1. Place the pork in the slow cooker and season it with black pepper.

2. In a small bowl, whisk together the hoisin, oyster sauce, soy sauce, rice wine vinegar, and garlic and pour over the pork. Cook on high for 4 hours or on low for 6 hours, until the pork is tender and falling apart.

3. Shred the pork and serve it on the flour tortillas topped with coleslaw, mushrooms, and scallions.

HELPFUL HINT If you can't find coleslaw mix, grab a head of green or red cabbage and cut into very thin slices.

2 pounds pork shoulder

Black pepper

½ cup hoisin sauce

2 tablespoons oyster sauce

2 tablespoons low-sodium soy sauce

2 tablespoons rice wine vinegar or sake

4 garlic cloves, minced

8 (6-inch) flour tortillas

1 (14-ounce) bag coleslaw mix

8 ounces shiitake mushrooms, sliced

2 scallions, sliced

Greek Veggie Flatbread

SERVES 4 | PREP TIME: 20 MIN | COOK TIME: 25 MIN

VEGETARIAN / NUT-FREE

These flatbreads are absolutely gorgeous with their vibrant summer colors. I've used individual naan (Indian flatbreads) as the base, but you can use whatever you prefer—pizza crusts, French bread, you name it.

1. Preheat the oven to 425°F.

2. Place the naan on a sheet pan and bake for 3 to 4 minutes, until crispy. Transfer to paper towels and set aside.

3. Spread the zucchini, bell pepper, and onion on the sheet pan and toss with the olive oil, salt, and pepper. Roast for 15 minutes, or until the zucchini is slightly browned.

4. Transfer the vegetables to a bowl and toss with the garlic, tomatoes, olives, oregano, and dill.

5. Line the sheet pan with parchment paper. Spread each naan with 1 tablespoon gournay cheese and place on the sheet pan. Top each naan with the vegetable mixture and garnish with feta.

6. Roast for 5 minutes. Season with additional salt and pepper and a squirt of lemon juice before serving.

IN SEASON NOW The oregano and dill really bring this dish to life, but if you can't find fresh herbs, you can always use dried. Just be sure to use less than the recipe calls for.

4 small naan

1 zucchini, diced

1 yellow bell pepper, diced

½ red onion, diced

2 tablespoons extra-virgin olive oil

Salt and black pepper

2 garlic cloves, minced

1 pint cherry tomatoes, halved

⅓ cup halved Kalamata olives

1 teaspoon chopped oregano

1 teaspoon chopped fresh dill

1 (5.2-ounce) package gournay cheese, such as Boursin

⅓ cup crumbled feta

Juice of ½ lemon

Greek Spinach Pie

SERVES 4 | PREP TIME: 15 MIN | COOK TIME: 25 MIN

VEGETARIAN / NUT-FREE

Also known as spanakopita, *this is one of Greece's most iconic dishes. Cheesy, briny feta and spinach wrapped in flaky buttered layers of phyllo—it requires a bit of time, but the end result is so worth it.*

1. Preheat the oven to 375°F. Lightly butter an 8-by-8-inch baking dish.

2. In a bowl, mix together the spinach, onion, feta, mozzarella, Parmesan, garlic, and nutmeg and season with salt and pepper.

3. Lay one sheet of phyllo dough in the baking dish and brush with some of the melted butter. Place a second sheet of phyllo on top and brush with butter, then place a third sheet on top.

4. Spread the spinach mixture on top of the phyllo dough.

5. Top the spinach mixture with three more layers of phyllo dough, brushing each with melted butter. Finish by brushing the top layer with butter.

6. Bake until golden brown, 20 to 22 minutes. Cool slightly before cutting into slices and serving.

HELPFUL HINT Phyllo dough is extremely thin, which means it can dry out very quickly and become brittle. To prevent that, cover the unused dough with a piece of plastic wrap and then a damp paper towel or cloth on top of it. The plastic wrap will prevent the damp towel from sticking to the dough, while the damp towel will keep the dough moist enough to use without breaking.

2 (10-ounce) packages frozen chopped spinach, thawed and dry

1 small onion, diced

½ cup crumbled feta

½ cup shredded mozzarella

½ cup grated Parmigiano-Reggiano

2 garlic cloves, minced

Pinch nutmeg

Salt and black pepper

1 (16-ounce) package frozen phyllo dough, thawed

4 tablespoons butter, melted, plus more (unmelted) for greasing the baking dish

Creamy Broccoli-Cheddar Quiche

SERVES 4 | PREP TIME: 30 MIN | COOK TIME: 50 MIN

VEGETARIAN / NUT-FREE

I think this quiche is one of the creamiest you will ever have. It's great for breakfast, lunch, or dinner, plus it's just as good at room temperature as it is heated up. Serve it with a side salad and your meal is complete.

1. Preheat the oven to 350°F.

2. Let the pie dough sit at room temperature for 30 minutes. Unroll the dough and line an oven-safe skillet with it.

3. Place the onion, garlic, and broccoli into the skillet and top with the Cheddar.

4. In a measuring cup, whisk together the eggs and milk and season with salt and pepper. Pour the mixture over the vegetables and bake for 45 minutes, or until the center is set.

HELPFUL HINT Place the skillet on a sheet pan just in case some of the filling spills out. It will prevent a possible mess in your oven.

1 (9-inch) refrigerated piecrust

1 onion, diced

1 garlic clove, minced

2 cups broccoli florets

1½ cups shredded Cheddar

4 large eggs, beaten

1½ cups milk

Salt and black pepper

Zucchini Noodle Pad Thai

SERVES 4 | PREP TIME: 10 MIN | COOK TIME: 6 MIN

DAIRY-FREE / GLUTEN-FREE

Love pad Thai, but can't do the noodles? Try my version that features spiralized zucchini instead. It's a nearly carb-free way to experience the same flavors of this classic dish from Thailand.

1. In a medium bowl, whisk together the peanut butter, chili paste, lime zest, fish sauce, and brown sugar. Set aside.

2. In a sauté pan over medium-high heat the olive oil and sauté the zoodles until softened, 3 to 4 minutes. Add the peanut butter mixture and the vegetable broth and cook, stirring, until heated through. Remove from the heat and add the lime juice, tomatoes, bean sprouts, and cilantro and stir to combine.

3. Garnish with peanuts, cilantro, and lime wedges and serve.

IN SEASON NOW Want to create an absolutely gorgeous dish? Try using half zucchini and half yellow squash zoodles.

4 tablespoons crunchy peanut butter

2 tablespoons chili paste

Zest and juice of 1 lime, divided

¼ cup fish sauce

1 tablespoon brown sugar

8 ounces zucchini zoodles

2 tablespoons extra-virgin olive oil

½ cup vegetable broth

½ cup cherry tomatoes, halved

1 cup mung bean sprouts

½ cup chopped fresh cilantro, plus more for garnish

2 tablespoons dry roasted peanuts, coarsely chopped

Lime wedges

Cheesy Polenta

SERVES 4 | PREP TIME: 5 MIN | COOK TIME: 10 MIN

GLUTEN-FREE / VEGETARIAN / NUT-FREE

You can eat this creamy, cheesy polenta all on its own, or it can be a base for roasted summer veggies or grilled chicken or shrimp. Try topping it with leftover vegetables for a quick balanced meal. When buying polenta, stay away from the quick-cook varieties. The pressure cooker will take care of that for you.

1. In an electric pressure cooker, combine the polenta and water and season with salt and pepper. Close and lock the lid, closing off the vent, and pressure cook on high for 10 minutes. Either allow the pressure cooker to depressurize naturally or carefully slide the quick release button.

2. Whisk in the Parmesan and Pecorino-Romano. Garnish with parsley and serve with extra cheese on the side, if desired.

ALT POT Polenta is more traditionally prepared in a Dutch oven. Simply bring the water to a boil and stir in the polenta, cooking it over medium heat until the polenta begins to thicken, about 5 minutes. Cover and cook on low for 30 minutes.

1 cup polenta

4 cups water

Salt and black pepper

1 cup grated
  Parmigiano-Reggiano

½ cup grated
  Pecorino-Romano

2 tablespoons chopped
  fresh Italian parsley

Linguine with Clam Sauce

SERVES 4 | PREP TIME: 10 MIN | COOK TIME: 18 MIN

DAIRY-FREE / NUT-FREE

When you eat a bowl filled with pasta and briny clam sauce, you'll be practically transported to a vacation day at the beach. Kick off your shoes, pour yourself a glass of crisp white wine, and relax.

1. Bring a large stockpot of salted water to a boil over high heat. Add the linguine and cook until al dente, 9 to 10 minutes. Drain in a colander and set aside.

2. Reduce the heat to medium, add the olive oil, garlic, red pepper flakes, anchovies, thyme, and oregano and cook for 2 minutes. Add the wine, canned clams, and littleneck clams, cover, and let steam for about 5 minutes, until the shells open. Discard any clams that do not open.

3. Add the butter, lemon zest and juice, and season the broth with salt and pepper. Serve over the hot linguine, garnished with parsley.

HELPFUL HINT Never cook any shellfish that is already open. That means they are dead and harmful to eat. Try tapping on their shells. If they close, they're safe to cook.

1 pound linguine

2 tablespoons extra-virgin olive oil

4 garlic cloves, minced

1 teaspoon red pepper flakes

6 anchovy fillets

1 teaspoon dried thyme

½ teaspoon dried oregano

¼ cup dry white wine

1 (6.5-ounce) can chopped clams

24 littleneck clams

3 tablespoons butter

Zest and juice of 1 lemon

Salt and black pepper

2 tablespoons chopped fresh parsley

Pesto Pasta with Shrimp and Crab

SERVES 4 | PREP TIME: 15 MIN | COOK TIME: 15 MIN

This dish is delicious served either hot or cold, which makes it ideal to take on a picnic or to a potluck. It's also impressive enough to serve company or as part of a buffet at a party. Everyone will love it.

1. Bring a Dutch oven filled with salted water to a boil over high heat. Add the pasta and cook until al dente, 8 to 9 minutes. Drain, cover, and set aside.

2. In a food processor, combine the basil, ½ cup Parmesan, garlic, pine nuts, red pepper flakes, salt, pepper, lemon juice, and olive oil and process until smooth.

3. Reheat the Dutch oven over medium heat, then add the butter and shrimp and cook until pink, 2 to 3 minutes. Add the cooked pasta and the pesto and toss to combine. Garnish with the crab and additional Parmesan cheese, if desired.

IN SEASON NOW Basil virtually grows like a weed, and one of the best ways to use it up is to make pesto. If you have extra, freeze it for next time!

8 ounces medium shell pasta

2 cups choppped fresh basil

½ to ¾ cup grated Parmigiano-Reggiano

2 garlic cloves

¼ cup toasted pine nuts

Pinch red pepper flakes

1 teaspoon salt

1 teaspoon black pepper

Juice of ½ lemon

⅓ cup extra-virgin olive oil

2 tablespoons butter

¾ pound shrimp (size 21/25), peeled and deveined

½ pound jumbo lump crabmeat

Szechuan Shrimp with Toasted Sesame Broccoli

SERVES 4 | PREP TIME: 10 MIN | COOK TIME: 15 MIN

DAIRY-FREE / GLUTEN-FREE / NUT-FREE

There is something very intoxicating about the smell of roasting sesame oil. Tossed with spicy shrimp and broccoli, it becomes even better. Adjust the red pepper flakes as needed, depending on how spicy you like it.

1. Preheat the oven to 400°F. Line a sheet pan with parchment paper.

2. Place the broccoli on one side of the pan and drizzle with the olive and sesame oils. Season with salt and pepper and roast for 10 minutes.

3. In a large bowl, toss the shrimp with the red pepper flakes and sesame-ginger dressing.

4. Add the shrimp to the other side of the sheet pan, sprinkle with sesame seeds, and roast for 5 minutes or until the shrimp turn pink. Garnish with scallions and serve.

HELPFUL HINT Cut the broccoli into small florets—not only will they cook faster, they'll look better alongside the shrimp.

1 head broccoli, cut into florets

2 tablespoons extra-virgin olive oil

2 teaspoons sesame oil

Salt and black pepper

1 pound shrimp (size 21/25), peeled and deveined

½ teaspoon red pepper flakes

½ cup sesame-ginger dressing

1 teaspoon sesame seeds

4 scallions, thinly sliced

Spanish Garlic Shrimp

SERVES 4 | PREP TIME: 8 MIN | COOK TIME: 10 MIN

NUT-FREE

I tried this dish at a Spanish restaurant in Maryland, and it was so good I had to stop myself from literally licking the plate. I think the smoked paprika is what makes my interpretation pretty irresistible.

1. In a medium bowl, toss the shrimp with the garlic, paprika, and red pepper flakes, then season with salt and pepper.

2. In a sauté pan over medium-high heat the olive oil and sear the shrimp until just cooked through, 1 to 2 minutes.

3. Add the sherry and cook, stirring to deglaze the pan. Add the tomatoes and lemon zest and cook for 5 minutes.

4. Add the butter and stir to combine. Season with additional salt and pepper to taste. Garnish with parsley and serve with toasted baguette slices.

VARIATION Sherry is native to Spain, so it makes sense to use it in this dish. But if you don't have any, a dry wine will work as well.

1 pound (21/25) shrimp, peeled, deveined

12 garlic cloves, minced

1 teaspoon smoked paprika

¾ teaspoon red pepper flakes

Salt and black pepper

1 tablespoon extra-virgin olive oil

4 ounces dry sherry

1 (28-ounce) can diced tomatoes

Zest of 1 lemon

2 tablespoons butter, cut into small pieces

2 tablespoons chopped fresh parsley

1 baguette, toasted and sliced

Southern Shrimp Boil

SERVES 4 | PREP TIME: 12 MIN | COOK TIME: 30 MIN

GLUTEN-FREE / NUT-FREE

This recipe serves four, which is fine for everyday, but a shrimp boil is even better with a crowd, so double or triple this recipe and invite all your friends over. This dish was made for a party.

1. Fill a Dutch oven with enough water to cover the potatoes by 1 inch. Bring to a boil over high heat and cook until the potatoes are fork-tender, 10 to 12 minutes. Add the corn during the last 5 minutes of cook time. Drain and set aside.

2. Reduce the heat to medium-high, add 1 tablespoon butter and cook the sausage for 5 to 6 minutes.

3. Add the shrimp, garlic, and the remaining 2 tablespoons butter and cook until the shrimp is pink, 2 to 3 minutes. Toss with the Old Bay seasoning.

4. Return the potatoes and corn to the pot and cook for 2 to 3 minutes or until heated through.

5. Serve in bowls, garnished with parsley and lemon wedges.

HELPFUL HINT If you don't want to heat up your kitchen, this can be cooked in a stockpot on your grill. In fact, if you're a real Southerner, you probably have a propane tank and stand you pull out just for this dish.

1 pound baby
  potatoes, halved
3 ears corn, each cut into
  3 pieces
3 tablespoons butter,
  divided
4 links andouille sausage,
  cut into 2-inch chunks
1 pound shrimp
  (size 21/25), peeled and
  deveined
6 garlic cloves, minced
4 tablespoons Old Bay
  seasoning
2 tablespoons chopped
  fresh parsley
1 lemon, cut into wedges

Grain Bowl with Salmon, Spinach, and Tomatoes

SERVES 4 | PREP TIME: 10 MIN | COOK TIME: 20 MIN

NUT-FREE

I love this dish because it has the perfect balance of vegetables, carbohydrates, and protein. Eating good food never tasted so guilt-free.

1. In a sauté pan, bring the water and a bit of salt to a boil. Stir in the couscous, turn off the heat, cover, and let sit for 5 minutes.

2. Using a fork, fluff the couscous and transfer it to a bowl. Cover to keep warm.

3. In the same sauté pan over medium-high heat, add 1 tablespoon olive oil, the garlic, and the spinach and cook until wilted, 1 to 2 minutes. Season with salt and pepper. Remove the spinach from the pan and set aside with the couscous to keep warm.

4. Add the remaining 1 tablespoon olive oil and the salmon to cook until nicely browned, 3 to 4 minutes. Flip and cook until browned, 3 to 4 minutes.

5. Add the wine and cook, stirring to deglaze the pan. Reduce the heat to low, add the butter and whisk to create a sauce. Season with salt and pepper to taste.

6. To serve, spoon couscous into four bowls, followed by the spinach to one side and salmon in the middle. Top with the tomatoes and drizzles of the sauce.

VARIATION To make this gluten-free, use rice instead of couscous. If you prefer to go dairy-free, simply omit the butter at the end.

1½ cups water

1 cup couscous

2 tablespoons extra-virgin olive oil, divided

2 garlic cloves, minced

1 pound chopped fresh spinach

Salt and black pepper

4 (6-ounce) salmon fillets

¼ cup dry white wine

2 tablespoons butter, cut into small pieces

1 cup halved grape tomatoes

Pan-Roasted Salmon with Tomato Vinaigrette

SERVES 4 | PREP TIME: 10 MIN | COOK TIME: 15 MIN

GLUTEN-FREE / NUT-FREE

This dish is as beautiful as it is delicious. Fresh tomatoes garnish a coral-colored salmon that all sits atop a bright bed of green spinach. Light, refreshing, and gorgeous.

1. In a sauté pan over medium-high heat 2 tablespoons olive oil, then add the spinach and cook until wilted. Add the garlic, season with salt and pepper, and cook for 30 seconds. Transfer the spinach to a plate and set aside.

2. In the same pan, add 1 tablespoon olive oil and the shallot and cook until softened, 3 to 4 minutes. Add the tomatoes and cook for 2 more minutes. Transfer to the plate with the spinach and set aside.

3. Add the remaining 1 tablespoon olive oil to the pan, add the salmon, and sear until lightly browned, 4 minutes per side.

4. Add the wine and cook, stirring to deglaze the pan, until about 1 tablespoon of liquid is left in the pan. Add the butter and whisk to create a sauce.

5. To serve, place spinach on each plate, top with a salmon fillet, and garnish each with shallots, tomatoes, and the sauce. Sprinkle with basil and a splash of balsamic vinegar.

HELPFUL HINT Fresh spinach cooks down to nearly nothing, so no need to feel daunted by the large volume needed for this recipe. It will be just enough for four servings.

4 tablespoons extra-virgin olive oil, divided

1 pound chopped fresh spinach

2 garlic cloves, minced

Salt and black pepper

1 shallot, sliced

1½ cups halved grape tomatoes

4 (6-ounce) salmon fillets

¼ cup dry white wine

2 tablespoons butter, cut into small pieces

1 tablespoon chopped fresh basil

1 teaspoon balsamic vinegar

Scallop, Tomato, and Basil Gratin

SERVES 4 | PREP TIME: 10 MIN | COOK TIME: 20 MIN

GLUTEN-FREE / NUT-FREE

Looking for the perfect date-night dinner that will really impress? This luscious but oh-so-easy gratin is just what you need to set the stage for the ultimate romantic evening. Serve it on its own, with a warm baguette on the side, or pile it over hot pasta. It's love at first bite.

1 pound scallops

2 tablespoons butter

2 garlic cloves, minced

¼ cup dry white wine

1 (14.5-ounce) can diced tomatoes

½ cup heavy cream

½ cup shredded mozzarella

2 tablespoons grated Parmigiano-Reggiano

2 tablespoons chopped fresh basil

Salt and black pepper

1. Pat the scallops with paper towels to dry them.

2. In a large sauté pan over medium-high heat, add the butter and scallops and sear until browned, 2 to 3 minutes. Flip and sear the other side until browned, 2 to 3 minutes.

3. Add the garlic and cook, stirring, for 30 seconds. Transfer the scallops to a plate.

4. Add the wine and cook, stirring to deglaze the pan. Add the tomatoes and simmer for 5 minutes.

5. Add the heavy cream and simmer until the liquid reduces, about 5 minutes.

6. Whisk in the mozzarella, Parmigiano-Reggiano, and basil. Season with salt and pepper and serve over the seared scallops.

VARIATION If scallops aren't your thing, substitute shrimp in this dish. Why not throw in some crab as well? They're in season during summer.

Rosemary-Lemon Salmon

SERVES 4 | PREP TIME: 5 MIN | COOK TIME: 1 TO 2 HOURS

DAIRY-FREE / GLUTEN-FREE / NUT-FREE / WORTH THE WAIT

Salmon, lemon, and rosemary, when combined, are more than the sum of their parts. Each complements the others, resulting in a dish that is highly satisfying in its simplicity. The slow cooker helps the salmon retain its moisture and avoid overcooking.

1. Place the salmon in a slow cooker and season with salt, pepper, and garlic. Top each fillet with 3 slices of lemon and a sprig of rosemary. Drizzle with the olive oil, then pour the wine over the top.

2. Cook on low for 1 to 2 hours. Serve hot.

ALT POT If you need to get dinner on the table a little faster, this dish is easily prepared on a sheet pan or in a sauté pan. Simply roast on a sheet pan for 12 minutes in a 400°F oven or sauté over medium-high heat in olive oil for 4 minutes per side.

4 (6-ounce) salmon fillets

Salt and black pepper

3 garlic cloves, minced

2 lemons, thinly sliced

2 (6-inch) rosemary sprigs, each cut in half

2 tablespoons extra-virgin olive oil

¼ cup dry white wine

Striped Bass with Ratatouille

SERVES 4 | PREP TIME: 15 MIN | COOK TIME: 20 MIN

DAIRY-FREE / GLUTEN-FREE / NUT-FREE

When you are looking for a light, fresh meal for a warm summer evening, you really should try this dish. Fresh fish is nestled among an array of seasonal veggies and herbs set off with pops of salty Kalamata olives.

1. Preheat the oven to 400°F. Line a sheet pan with parchment paper.

2. Arrange the zucchini, eggplant, onion, garlic, and tomatoes on the sheet pan. Top with the fish and season everything with salt, pepper, and thyme.

3. Drizzle with the olive oil and roast for 10 to 12 minutes.

4. Add the olives and roast for 5 more minutes. Garnish with the basil and serve.

VARIATION If you can't find or don't like striped bass, substitute any other fish in this recipe. Just remember that cooking times will vary depending on the thickness of the fish—thinner fish will take less time; thicker fish will take longer.

1 zucchini, diced

1 small eggplant, peeled and diced

1 onion, diced

2 garlic cloves, minced

1 (14.5-ounce) can diced tomatoes, drained, juices reserved

4 (6-ounce) striped bass fillets

Salt and black pepper

2 teaspoons dried thyme

2 tablespoons extra-virgin olive oil

½ cup Kalamata olives, pitted

½ cup chopped fresh basil

Fried Chicken

SERVES 6 | PREP TIME: 10 MIN | COOK TIME: 1 HOUR

DAIRY-FREE / NUT-FREE

*Some folks think that Southern fried chicken will
be difficult to make, but nothing could be further
from the truth. The hardest part is having enough
patience to wait for the crispy chicken to cool
before diving in.*

1. In a large Dutch oven, heat the vegetable oil to 350°F.

2. Season the chicken with salt and pepper.

3. In a large freezer bag, shake together the flour, salt, pepper, garlic and onion powders, paprika, and cayenne pepper. Dredge each piece of chicken in the seasoned flour and then place half of the chicken in the hot oil. The oil should come at least half way up the chicken.

4. Fry the chicken for 10 minutes, flip and fry the other side until well browned, another 10 minutes. The chicken is done when an instant-read thermometer placed in the thickest part of the chicken reads 165°F. Remove the chicken from the fat and drain on a paper towel–lined plate. Season with additional salt immediately and serve.

4 cups vegetable oil

1 fryer chicken, cut
   into pieces

2 tablespoons salt,
   plus more to season
   the chicken

2 tablespoons black
   pepper, plus more to
   season the chicken

2 cups all-purpose flour

1 tablespoon garlic powder

1 tablespoon onion powder

2 teaspoons paprika

1 teaspoon
   cayenne pepper

HELPFUL HINT You are going to have to cook the chicken
in batches so you don't overcrowd the pan and bring down
the temperature of the oil. If the oil cools off too much, the
chicken will absorb it and become really greasy instead
of crispy.

Honey and Spice Barbecue Chicken

SERVES 4 | PREP TIME: 15 MIN | COOK TIME: 35 MIN

DAIRY-FREE / NUT-FREE

Sometimes only sticky, sweet, spicy barbecue will do for dinner. When you bake this in the oven instead of on a grill, you get the same flavors without worrying about whether it's going to rain.

1. Preheat the oven to 350°F.

2. Rub the chicken with olive oil and season with salt and pepper. Place the chicken in a 9-by-13-inch baking dish and bake for 30 minutes.

3. In a measuring cup, combine the ketchup, brown sugar, honey, Worcestershire sauce, mustard, vinegar, ginger, ½ teaspoon black pepper, hot sauce, and liquid smoke to make the sauce.

4. Slather the sauce on the chicken and continue to bake for 5 more minutes or until a instant-read thermometer inserted into the thickest part of the breast reads 165°F.

HELPFUL HINT When you insert the thermometer into the chicken, go in from the side rather than the top. You'll get a much more accurate reading.

1 fryer chicken, cut into pieces

2 tablespoons extra-virgin olive oil

Salt

½ teaspoon black pepper, plus more for seasoning

1½ cups ketchup

3 tablespoons packed brown sugar

3 tablespoons honey

2 tablespoons Worcestershire sauce

2 tablespoons yellow mustard

2 tablespoons apple cider vinegar

½ teaspoon ground ginger

½ teaspoon hot sauce

1 teaspoon liquid smoke

Creamy Tuscan Garlic Chicken

SERVES 4 | PREP TIME: 20 MIN | COOK TIME: 30 MIN

NUT-FREE

This classic rustic dish from Italy is heartwarming, filling, and comes together easily for a quick week-night meal. Be sure to have plenty of bread on hand to soak up the irresistible sauce.

1. Bring a large sauté pan of salted water to a boil over high heat. Add the linguine and cook until al dente, 12 to 14 minutes. Drain in a colander and set aside in a warmed serving bowl.

2. Season the chicken with Italian seasoning, salt, and pepper. Pour the oil into the sauté pan, reduce the heat to medium-high, then add the chicken and cook until browned, 4 to 5 minutes per side. Transfer the chicken to a plate.

3. Add the garlic, heavy cream, chicken stock, and Parmesan to the pan and whisk until it starts to thicken. Add the spinach and sun-dried tomatoes and simmer until the spinach wilts. Add the chicken back to the pan and cook for 5 more minutes.

4. Serve over the hot linguine with extra Parmesan on the side, if desired.

VARIATION Don't feel like waiting for the chicken to thaw out? Try using shrimp instead.

1 pound linguine

1½ pounds skinless, boneless chicken breasts, thinly sliced

1 teaspoon Italian seasoning

Salt and black pepper

2 tablespoons extra-virgin olive oil

3 garlic cloves, minced

1 cup heavy cream

½ cup low-sodium chicken stock

½ cup grated Parmigiano-Reggiano

1 cup chopped fresh spinach

½ cup diced sun-dried tomatoes

Chicken Taverna

SERVES 4 | PREP TIME: 15 MIN | COOK TIME: 35 MIN

GLUTEN-FREE / NUT-FREE

Need a mini getaway? Try this dish—it will make you feel like you've been transported to the sunny country of Greece. Artichoke hearts and zucchini mingle with plenty of oregano, dill, and feta in every bite.

1. Season the chicken with salt and pepper. In a large sauté pan over medium-high heat, add the reserved artichoke marinade and the chicken and cook for 8 to 10 minutes, flipping once to brown both sides evenly. Transfer the chicken to a plate.

2. Add the tomatoes, zucchini, and onion to the pan and cook until softened, 3 to 4 minutes. Add the garlic, oregano, dill, and artichoke hearts and cook for 30 seconds.

3. Add the wine and cook, stirring to deglaze the pan.

4. Return the chicken to the pan, cover, and simmer for 15 minutes. Uncover and cook for 5 more minutes.

5. Season with salt and pepper to taste, garnish with feta cheese, and serve.

IN SEASON NOW Fresh herbs abound in the summer months. If you use fresh, remember to use three times as much fresh as you would dried. Add them just before you serve the dish for maximum flavor.

4 skinless, boneless chicken breasts

Salt and black pepper

1 (6-ounce) jar artichoke hearts, drained, marinade reserved

1 (28-ounce) can diced tomatoes

2 small zucchini, diced

1 onion, diced

3 garlic cloves, minced

1 teaspoon dried oregano

½ teaspoon dried dill

¼ cup dry red wine

⅓ cup crumbled feta

Peanut Chicken

SERVES 4 | PREP TIME: 10 MIN | COOK TIME: 3 TO 8 HOURS

DAIRY-FREE / GLUTEN-FREE / WORTH THE WAIT

What is it about the combination of peanut butter and classic Asian ingredients like soy sauce and ginger that makes it so darn good? Here I've used the slow cooker to meld those flavors with chicken, creating a warm and cozy meal. Serve with a sprinkle of chopped scallions and some naan or pita bread, and you'll have some very happy diners.

1. Place the chicken breasts in the slow cooker. Season lightly with salt and pepper.

2. In a measuring cup, whisk together the peanut butter, wine, soy sauce, ginger, garlic, vinegar, peanut oil, and red pepper flakes. Pour over the chicken and cook on high for 3 to 4 hours or on low for 6 to 8 hours.

3. Garnish with chopped scallions.

HELPFUL HINT If the sauce appears too thick, add a bit of water or stock to thin it.

4 skinless, boneless
   chicken breasts

Salt and black pepper

½ cup peanut butter

½ cup dry white wine

2 tablespoons low-sodium
   soy sauce

1 tablespoon grated ginger

2 garlic cloves, minced

1 tablespoon white or rice
   wine vinegar

2 tablespoons peanut oil

½ teaspoon red
   pepper flakes

4 scallions, chopped

Chicken and Veggie Kabobs

SERVES 4 | PREP TIME: 20 MIN | COOK TIME: 15 MIN

DAIRY-FREE / GLUTEN-FREE / NUT-FREE

Who needs a campfire to eat dinner on a stick?
These kabobs roast deliciously in the oven, needing
only a slice of rustic bread to make this filling meal.

1. Preheat the oven to 375°F. Line a sheet pan with parchment paper.

2. In a large bowl, combine the chicken, olive oil, garlic, thyme, smoked paprika, and salt and pepper.

3. Alternately thread the chicken and vegetables onto metal or wooden skewers. Place the kabobs on the pan and pour any remaining marinade over the chicken.

4. Roast for 12 to 15 minutes, turning occasionally for even browning. Serve with lemon wedges.

HELPFUL HINT If you are using wooden skewers it's a good idea to soak them in water for at least 30 minutes before you use them. While it's a bigger issue when grilling the kabobs, it will help prevent them from burning in the oven.

1½ pounds skinless, boneless chicken breasts, cut into 1-inch cubes

3 tablespoons extra-virgin olive oil

4 garlic cloves, minced

1 teaspoon dried thyme

½ teaspoon smoked paprika

Salt and black pepper

½ pound whole button mushrooms, trimmed

2 onions, cut into wedges

1 pound cherry tomatoes

1 green bell pepper, cut into 1-inch pieces

1 yellow squash, cut into ½-inch slices

1 lemon, cut into wedges

Chicken Molé

SERVES 4 | PREP TIME: 20 MIN | COOK TIME: 4 TO 8 HOURS

DAIRY-FREE / GLUTEN-FREE / WORTH THE WAIT
The secret ingredient in a great molé is chocolate—in this case, unsweetened cocoa. It's a classic way to add richness and depth of flavor without sweetness. Serve on corn tortillas with your favorite toppings.

1. Season the chicken with salt and pepper and place in the slow cooker.

2. In a food processor, combine the chicken stock, onion, garlic, chipotle pepper, tomato paste, almonds, raisins, cocoa, cumin, and cinnamon and process until smooth. Spread over the chicken, cover, and cook on low for 8 hours, or on high for 4 hours, until chicken is tender.

HELPFUL HINT Be sure to puree the seasoning mixture well, particularly the almonds, so you don't end up with a gritty texture.

4 skinless, boneless chicken thighs

Salt and black pepper

½ cup low-sodium chicken stock

1 onion, quartered

4 garlic cloves

1 chipotle pepper in adobo sauce

2 tablespoons tomato paste

¼ cup almonds

¼ cup raisins

2 tablespoons unsweetened cocoa

1 tablespoon ground cumin

1 teaspoon ground cinnamon

Basque Chicken

SERVES 4 | PREP TIME: 20 MIN | COOK TIME: 30 MIN

DAIRY-FREE / GLUTEN-FREE / NUT-FREE

Inspired by the Basque region of Spain, this chicken dish is bursting with flavor. From the smoked paprika and sherry vinegar to the stuffed olives and hearty tomatoes, this dish is a celebration of Spanish cuisine.

1. Preheat the pressure cooker on sauté. Season the chicken with salt and pepper. Add the olive oil and chicken to the pot and sear until browned, 8 minutes per side. Add the potatoes and onion and cook for 5 minutes. Add the garlic and cook for 30 seconds. Turn off the sauté function.

2. Add the tomatoes, tomato paste, red peppers, olives, smoked paprika, and vinegar to the pressure cooker. Close and lock the lid, closing off the vent, and pressure cook on high for 10 minutes. Either allow the pressure cooker to depressurize naturally or carefully slide the quick release button.

3. Remove the chicken from the pot. If necessary, set the pressure cooker to sauté and reduce the sauce until thickened. Season with salt and pepper to taste and serve over the chicken.

ALT POT This dish would also be delicious prepared in a Dutch oven. Follow step 1 and then cover the Dutch oven and place it in a 350°F oven for 1 hour, or until the chicken is cooked through and registers 165°F with an instant-read thermometer.

6 bone-in, skin-on chicken thighs

Salt and black pepper

2 tablespoons extra-virgin olive oil

1 pound baby potatoes, halved

1 onion, thinly sliced

4 garlic cloves, minced

1 (14-ounce) can stewed tomatoes

2 tablespoons tomato paste

1 cup sliced roasted red peppers

½ cup pimento-stuffed green olives

2 teaspoons smoked paprika

1 tablespoon sherry vinegar

Steamed Mussels with Spicy Chorizo

SERVES 4 | PREP TIME: 10 MIN | COOK TIME: 12 MIN

DAIRY-FREE / NUT-FREE

Steamed mussels and spicy sausage are the perfect vacation meal. As you savor the aromatic shellfish with its savory wine-based sauce, you'll feel like you've spent the day at the beach, without the sand in your shorts.

1. Rinse the mussels well under cold water. Pull off any beards and discard any mussels that are broken or gaping open.

2. In a large stockpot over medium-high heat, cook the sausage until browned, 4 to 5 minutes.

3. Add the shallot and garlic and cook for 30 seconds. Add the wine and cook, stirring to deglaze the pan, until nearly evaporated.

4. Add in the tomatoes, tomato paste, red pepper flakes, and mussels. Cover and cook on high for 2 minutes. Remove the lid and toss the mussels well with a large spoon. Cover and cook until the mussels have opened wide, another 2 minutes.

5. Add the butter, stirring to combine. Garnish with parsley and season with salt and pepper. Serve with the toasted baguette slices.

3½ to 4 pounds mussels

1 pound chorizo sausage, casing removed

1 shallot, diced

6 garlic cloves, minced

½ cup dry white wine

1 (14.5-ounce) can diced tomatoes

1 tablespoon tomato paste

½ teaspoon red pepper flakes

2 tablespoons butter, cut into pieces

2 tablespoons chopped fresh parsley

Salt and black pepper

1 baguette, sliced and toasted

HELPFUL HINT Mussels have what's called a "beard." It's black and hair-like and found often protruding from between the two shells. As you're scrubbing the mussels, simply pull the beard to remove it. It might require a little tug to break it free.

Blackberry-Roasted Pork Tenderloin

SERVES 4 | PREP TIME: 8 MIN | COOK TIME: 45 MIN

DAIRY-FREE / GLUTEN-FREE / NUT-FREE

Freshly picked blackberries are one of the greatest treats of summer. But you can also use fresh raspberries or even raspberry jam if fresh berries aren't in season or are hard to get.

1. Preheat the oven to 400°F. Line a sheet pan with parchment paper.

2. Place the pork on one side of the sheet pan and the potatoes on the other. Drizzle both with olive oil and season with salt and pepper.

3. Roast for 25 to 30 minutes, until the pork registers an internal temperature of 145°F, and the potatoes are fork-tender.

4. In a small bowl, whisk together the garlic, jam, and balsamic vinegar. Pour it over the cooked pork along with the blackberries. Return the pork to the oven and roast for 5 minutes.

5. Remove the pork from the oven, cover with aluminum foil, and let rest for 10 minutes before cutting into slices. Serve with the roasted potatoes.

HELPFUL HINT Don't be tempted to brush the sauce on when you first put the pork in the oven. The sugar in the jam will burn while cooking. Wait until just before you're ready to serve it to brush on the tenderloin.

1½ pounds pork tenderloin

1 pound baby potatoes, quartered

1 tablespoon extra-virgin olive oil

Salt and black pepper

3 garlic cloves, minced

½ cup seedless blackberry jam

2 tablespoons balsamic vinegar

½ pint blackberries

Braised Brisket with Bourbon-Peach Glaze

SERVES 4 | PREP TIME: 15 MIN | COOK TIME: 3 HOURS 30 MIN

DAIRY-FREE / GLUTEN-FREE / NUT-FREE / WORTH THE WAIT

Adding bourbon to a recipe is pretty common in Southern cooking. By cooking it with the brisket in a Dutch oven and slow cooking for a few hours, the alcohol burns away, leaving the smooth sweet flavors that go so well with peaches. The resulting brisket is sweet, savory, and sublime.

1. Preheat the oven to 350°F.

2. Season the brisket with salt and pepper. In a Dutch oven over medium-high heat the olive oil, add the brisket, and cook until browned, 8 to 10 minutes per side.

3. Add ½ cup bourbon and cook, stirring to deglaze the pan. Add the beef stock, garlic, and thyme and stir to combine.

4. Cover and bake for 3 hours, or until the meat is very tender. Transfer the brisket to a plate.

5. Carefully return the Dutch oven to the stovetop and, over high heat, cook the liquid in the pot until it reduces to about 1 cup.

6. In a measuring cup, whisk together the preserves, the remaining ½ cup bourbon, and chipotle powder.

1 (4-pound) flat cut beef brisket

Salt and black pepper

2 tablespoons extra-virgin olive oil

1 cup bourbon, divided

2 cups low-sodium beef stock

3 garlic cloves, minced

1 tablespoon dried thyme

½ cup peach preserves

½ teaspoon chipotle powder

7. Pour the mixture into the reduced liquid in the Dutch oven and whisk to combine. Cook for 5 minutes and season with additional salt and pepper to taste.

8. Return the brisket to the Dutch oven, coat with the sauce, and cook for 5 more minutes. Serve.

IN SEASON NOW The preserves give this sauce a nice body, but don't be afraid to dice up some fresh peaches and add them just before you serve the brisket for added flavor and texture.

Baby Back Ribs

SERVES 4 | PREP TIME: 15 MIN | COOK TIME: 40 MIN

DAIRY-FREE / GLUTEN-FREE / NUT-FREE

This recipe is literally life-changing. That may sound extreme, but if you've ever spent all day (or more!) making ribs, you'll be thrilled that this method ensures they'll be ready in less than 1 hour. What are you going to do with all that extra time? Eat more ribs!

1. In a small bowl, mix together the brown sugar, smoked paprika, salt, pepper, chili powder, onion powder, and cayenne to make a dry rub.

2. Remove the membrane from the boney side of the ribs. Liberally season both sides of the ribs with the dry rub.

3. Place the rack that came with your pressure cooker inside the cooker. Pour the water, vinegar, and liquid smoke into the pressure cooker. Place the seasoned ribs on top of the rack, bending them into a circle so they are standing up on their side.

4. Close and lock the lid, closing off the vent, and pressure cook on high for 35 minutes. Either allow the pressure cooker to depressurize naturally or carefully slide the quick release button.

¾ cup packed brown sugar

½ cup smoked paprika

2½ tablespoons salt

2½ tablespoons black pepper

1½ tablespoons chili powder

1½ tablespoons onion powder

1 teaspoon cayenne pepper

1 rack baby back ribs

½ cup water

½ cup apple cider vinegar

¼ teaspoon liquid smoke

1 cup barbecue sauce

5. Remove the ribs from the pressure cooker and slather them with your favorite barbecue sauce.

6. For the best flavor, place the ribs on an oven-proof serving tray and pop under the broiler for 4 minutes before serving.

ALT POT If you're not going to use the pressure cooker or the grill, you can always spread the ribs out on a sheet pan. I like to season them with the dry rub and then wrap them tightly in aluminum foil. Bake them at 300°F for 2 hours. Cool completely, refrigerate overnight and then reheat in a 400°F oven for 12 minutes. Brush on the barbecue sauce and broil for 4 minutes.

FALL

As the weather starts to cool down, an amazing array of vegetables are ready to harvest. The season calls for warm and spicy stews and soups, along with hearty snacks to enjoy while watching football games. At the markets, look for pumpkins and butternut squash, apples, Brussels sprouts, and root vegetables. Dishes will often have a little more spice, which will make everyone feel cozier after an afternoon of raking leaves or hiking through the woods.

CHICKEN BREASTS

Loaded Baked Potato Skins

SERVES 4 | PREP TIME: 12 MIN | COOK TIME: 35 MIN

GLUTEN-FREE / NUT-FREE

Everyone loves potato skins but, let's be honest, the potato skins are just the vehicle to eat bacon and cheese. Even though that's probably true, when the potatoes are browned and crunchy and topped with sour cream and chives, you'll eat every bit of them.

1. Preheat the oven to 400°F.

2. Place the bacon in 9-by-13-inch baking dish and bake for 12 to 15 minutes or until crispy. Transfer to a paper towel. Wipe out any excess fat from the baking dish. Crumble the bacon.

3. Prick the potatoes all over with a fork and microwave on high for 5 minutes. Turn them over and microwave for 4 more minutes, or until the potatoes have softened.

4. Let the potatoes cool slightly. Cut them in half lengthwise and scoop out the inside, leaving at least ¼ inch of flesh in the skin. Season with salt and pepper. Brush the insides with the melted butter and sprinkle with the garlic.

5. Place in the baking dish and bake for 10 minutes, or until lightly browned. Top with crumbled bacon and cheese. Bake for 4 minutes, or until the cheese melts.

6. Serve with sour cream and chives.

HELPFUL HINT Be sure to use russet potatoes for this dish. Their boat-like shape will make a pretty presentation when you serve them. And don't throw the filling away after you scoop it out. Save it to make mashed potatoes for another night.

4 strips bacon

4 russet potatoes

Salt and black pepper

4 tablespoons butter, melted

4 garlic cloves, minced

1½ cups shredded Cheddar

½ cup sour cream

2 tablespoons chopped fresh chives

Barbecue Bourbon Chicken Wings

SERVES 4 | PREP TIME: 5 MIN | COOK TIME: 3 TO 6 HOURS

DAIRY-FREE / GLUTEN-FREE / NUT-FREE / WORTH THE WAIT

Who doesn't love a good old-fashioned chicken wing bathed in barbecue sauce? And the only thing any better is a splash of your favorite bourbon to send these wings over the top. This would be a good time to find something constructive to do instead of watching the clock until they are done.

1. Place the chicken in the slow cooker and season with salt and pepper.

2. Pour the barbecue sauce and bourbon over the top of the chicken and stir to coat.

3. Cook on high for 3 to 4 hours or on low for 6 hours. Serve hot.

2 pounds chicken wings
Salt and black pepper
1½ cups barbecue sauce
2½ tablespoons bourbon

VARIATION Not a huge bourbon fan? Try adding a bit of rum instead.

Chili

SERVES 4 | PREP TIME: 10 MIN | COOK TIME: 45 MIN

DAIRY-FREE / GLUTEN-FREE / NUT-FREE

Sometimes nothing but a steaming pot of chili will do for dinner. The longer it cooks, the better it tastes. It's even better the next day. Serve with the toppings of your choice: tortilla chips, corn bread, shredded cheese, sour cream, or Greek yogurt.

1. In a stockpot over medium-high heat, cook the ground beef until browned, 6 to 8 minutes.

2. Add the onion, bell pepper, and jalapeño and cook until softened. Add the garlic and cook for 30 seconds.

3. Add the black beans, tomatoes, chili powder, cumin, and cayenne, bring to a boil, and cook for 2 minutes. Lower the heat to medium and simmer for 30 minutes.

4. Season with salt and pepper to taste. Garnish with the toppings of your choice.

VARIATION We used ground beef in our chili, but you can also substitute spicy sausage, ground turkey, or the new plant-based substitutes, depending on the flavor you're going for.

1 pound ground beef

1 onion, diced

1 green bell pepper, diced

1 jalapeño, minced

4 garlic cloves, minced

1 (15.5-ounce) can black beans, drained and rinsed

1 (28-ounce) can diced tomatoes

2 tablespoons chili powder

1 tablespoon ground cumin

Pinch cayenne pepper

Salt and black pepper

Creamy Bacon Soup

SERVES 4 | PREP TIME: 12 MIN | COOK TIME: 25 MIN

GLUTEN-FREE / NUT-FREE

This recipe takes a simple potato soup and elevates it to something absolutely elegant. The richness of the gournay cheese is sublime. Pair it with a full-bodied white wine and a great baguette, and dinner is served.

1. In a stockpot over medium-high heat, cook the bacon until crisp. Transfer to a paper towel. Reserve 1 tablespoon of the drippings and crumble the bacon.

2. Add the onion to the pot and cook until softened, 4 to 5 minutes. Add the garlic and cook 30 seconds.

3. Add the chicken stock and potatoes, bring to a boil, and cook for 2 minutes. Lower the heat to medium and simmer until the potatoes are tender, 8 to 10 minutes.

4. Using an immersion blender, puree the soup until smooth.

5. Whisk in the gournay cheese and season with salt and pepper to taste.

6. Serve garnished with crumbled bacon and chives.

4 strips bacon

1 small onion, diced

3 garlic cloves, minced

5 cups low-sodium chicken stock

2 pounds russet or Yukon Gold potatoes, peeled and diced

1 (5.2-ounce) package gournay cheese, such as Boursin

Salt and black pepper

1 tablespoon chopped fresh chives

VARIATION Gournay, a soft, herbed cheese is easy to find in most stores, but if you prefer to use Cheddar, that will work as well. Just be sure to buy a block and shred it yourself. Pre-shredded cheese contains cellulose to prevent the cheese from caking. It will make your soup gritty.

Clam Chowder

SERVES 4 | PREP TIME: 15 MIN | COOK TIME: 30 MIN

NUT-FREE

The smokiness of bacon and the brininess of clams is a perfect pairing. Just don't add the clams too early or let them cook too long; otherwise they'll become really tough and chewy. Then get some great bread, a side salad, and a creamy Chardonnay to round out your meal.

1. In a Dutch oven over medium-high heat, cook the bacon until crispy. Transfer to a paper towel and reserve the bacon fat in the pot. Crumble the bacon and set aside.

2. Add the onion and celery to the pot and cook until softened, 5 minutes. Add the garlic and cook 30 seconds.

3. Sprinkle in the flour and whisk, cooking for 2 minutes. Pour in the clam juice, chicken stock, and half-and-half, whisking well to incorporate. Bring to a boil and cook until the mixture thickens, about 2 minutes.

4. Reduce the heat to medium, add the potatoes and thyme, and simmer until the potatoes are tender, 12 to 14 minutes.

5. Add the clams along with their juice and stir to combine. Season with salt and pepper to taste, garnish with bacon, and serve.

IN SEASON NOW If you can get fresh clams, by all means use them. Steam them first, remove the meat from the shells, and add them to the chowder in step 5.

4 strips bacon
1 small onion, diced
4 celery stalks, diced
3 garlic cloves, minced
¼ cup all-purpose flour
1 (8-ounce) bottle
   clam juice
1 cup low-sodium
   chicken stock
2 cups half-and-half
2 large red potatoes, diced
1 teaspoon dried thyme
2 (6.5-ounce) cans
   chopped clams
Salt and black pepper

Gumbo

SERVES 4 | PREP TIME: 12 MIN | COOK TIME: 1 HOUR

DAIRY-FREE / NUT-FREE / WORTH THE WAIT

Wishing you were dining in New Orleans? This steaming pot of gumbo—with its smoky sausage, chicken, and spices—is just the thing to transport you there in spirit.

1. In a stockpot over medium-high heat the olive oil, add the chicken, and cook until it is well browned, 6 to 8 minutes.

2. Add in the celery, bell pepper, onion, and okra and cook until the onion is translucent and most of the liquid has evaporated, 4 to 6 minutes. Add the garlic and cook for 30 seconds.

3. Sprinkle the flour over the vegetables and cook, stirring, for 2 minutes.

4. Add the chicken stock, tomatoes, and sausage, bring to a boil, and cook, stirring, for 2 minutes. Lower the heat to medium and simmer for 45 minutes.

5. Add the smoked paprika and hot sauce and season with salt and pepper to taste.

HELPFUL HINT Andouille is a spicy sausage very traditional to this dish, but if you can't find it, any well-seasoned sausage will do.

2 tablespoons extra-virgin olive oil

4 skinless, boneless chicken thighs, cut into 1-inch cubes

2 celery stalks, diced

1 green bell pepper, diced

1 onion, diced

2 cups frozen cut okra

4 garlic cloves, minced

2 tablespoons all-purpose flour

4 cups low-sodium chicken stock

2 (14.5-ounce) cans stewed tomatoes

8 ounces andouille sausage, thinly sliced

1 tablespoon smoked paprika

½ tablespoon hot sauce

Salt and black pepper

Spicy Pumpkin Soup

SERVES 4 | PREP TIME: 5 MIN | COOK TIME: 3 TO 5 HOURS

GLUTEN-FREE / NUT-FREE / WORTH THE WAIT

Long before the pumpkin spice craze took over, there was this soup. Creamy and elegant, you can make it as spicy or as tame as you like. It's like autumn in a bowl.

1. Combine the onion, garlic, curry powder, coriander, cayenne pepper, pumpkin puree, chicken stock, half-and-half, and brown sugar in a slow cooker and mix well. Cook on high for 3 hours or on low for 5 hours.

2. Season with salt and pepper to taste and serve hot.

HELPFUL HINT Make sure you pick up 100-percent pure pureed pumpkin, not pumpkin pie filling. The two are very different. The latter is much sweeter with lots of added sugar.

1 onion, diced

2 garlic cloves, minced

2 teaspoons curry powder

1 teaspoon ground coriander

⅛ teaspoon cayenne pepper

1 (15-ounce) can pumpkin puree

2½ cups low-sodium chicken stock

1 cup half-and-half

¼ cup light brown sugar

Salt and black pepper

Meatball Subs

SERVES 4 | PREP TIME: 8 MIN | COOK TIME: 20 MIN

NUT-FREE

These subs are a great second-night meal. Start by making a double batch of the meatballs, one for spaghetti and meatballs and the other to make these subs the next night. Two nights of dinner is done.

1. Preheat the oven to 400°F. Line a sheet pan with parchment paper.

2. In a large bowl, mix together the sausage, ground beef, garlic powder, bread, milk, egg, and Parmesan and season with salt and pepper. Using an ice cream scoop, form the mixture into meatballs.

3. Place the meatballs on the sheet pan and roast for 10 to 12 minutes or until they are fully cooked. Transfer the meatballs to a plate. Drain any fat from the pan and replace the parchment paper with a fresh sheet.

4. In a microwave-safe bowl, microwave the marinara sauce for 2 minutes, until hot.

5. Place the meatballs in the sub rolls and top with marinara sauce and provolone slices. Place the subs on the sheet pan and bake for 5 to 6 minutes or until the cheese melts.

½ pound spicy
Italian sausage

½ pound lean ground beef

2 teaspoons garlic powder

2 slices bread, torn
into pieces

¼ cup milk

1 large egg, beaten

¼ cup grated
Parmigiano-Reggiano

Salt and black pepper

4 sub rolls, split

1 (24-ounce) jar
marinara sauce

6 slices provolone

VARIATION Ground turkey or meat substitutes would be really nice in these meatballs.

Pepperoni Calzones

SERVES 4 | PREP TIME: 20 MIN | COOK TIME: 35 MIN

NUT-FREE

Pizzas are great, but sometimes you just want it all in one neat little package. With premade dough, this dinner can be done in a flash. If you make more of these than you need, freeze them before you bake them, and then just pop them into the oven the next time you're craving calzones.

1. Preheat the oven to 400°F. Line a sheet pan with parchment paper.

2. Place the bell pepper and onion on the sheet pan and bake for 10 to 12 minutes or until they have softened. Drain them in a colander to remove any excess liquid.

3. Divide each ball of dough in half. On a lightly floured surface, roll each half out into a 10-inch circle. In the middle of each circle, spread ⅓ cup marinara, a quarter of the pepper-onion mixture, a quarter of the pepperoni, and ½ cup cheese.

4. Gently fold the dough in half so it resembles a half moon. Carefully fold the edges of the dough up and press together to seal in the filling. Place the calzones on the sheet pan.

5. Using a sharp knife, cut two vent holes in the top of each calzone. Brush lightly with olive oil and bake for 20 minutes or until golden brown.

1 green bell pepper, diced

½ onion, diced

2 balls (12 ounces) pizza dough

2 cups marinara sauce

4 ounces sliced pepperoni

2 cups shredded mozzarella cheese

1 tablespoon extra-virgin olive oil

IN SEASON NOW If you prefer a more plant-based calzone, skip the pepperoni and substitute mushrooms. They bring a meatiness that is perfect for this dish.

Smoked Provolone and Prosciutto Pizza

SERVES 4 | PREP TIME: 6 MIN | COOK TIME: 12 MIN

NUT-FREE

Who says you need a sauce to make a great pizza? This one will have you seeing stars—as in under the Tuscan sky kind of stars. You can always make your own dough, but for those nights when you just want to eat fast, keep some prepared pizza dough on hand.

1. Preheat the oven to 450°F. Line a sheet pan with parchment paper.

2. Roll out or press the pizza dough onto the sheet pan.

3. In a small bowl, combine the olive oil and garlic and brush it on the pizza dough.

4. Top with the provolone, red pepper flakes, and Parmesan.

5. Bake for 8 minutes or until the crust is browned.

6. Top with the prosciutto and bake for another 4 minutes.

7. Garnish with basil, drizzle with balsamic vinegar, and season with salt and pepper. Cut into slices and serve.

HELPFUL HINT If you don't want to use a sheet pan, you can always bake the pizza directly on a pizza stone or steel. The texture will be more like take-out pizzas.

1 (12-ounce) container refrigerated pizza dough

1 tablespoon extra-virgin olive oil

2 garlic cloves, minced

8 ounces sliced provolone

½ teaspoon red pepper flakes

½ cup grated Parmigiano-Reggiano

2 ounces thinly sliced prosciutto

2 tablespoons thinly sliced fresh basil

Balsamic vinegar

Salt and black pepper

Honeycrisp, Bacon, and Brie Grilled Cheese

SERVES 4 | PREP TIME: 8 MIN | COOK TIME: 18 MIN

NUT-FREE

The cheesier the better I always say. If you want to be sure your sandwich doesn't fall apart when you flip it, put cheese on both the top and bottom. As it melts, it will be the glue that holds it together.

1. In a skillet over medium-high heat, cook the bacon until crispy, 6 to 8 minutes. Transfer to a paper towel, but reserve the fat in the pan.

2. Assemble the sandwiches by placing the Brie on top of one slice of bread followed by the apple slices, honey, and the bacon. Top with the second slice of bread.

3. In the skillet over medium heat, place two sandwiches, cheese-side down, cover, and cook until the bottom browns and the cheese begins to melt, 4 to 5 minutes.

4. Flip the sandwiches over and cook until browned, 4 to 5 minutes.

5. Repeat with the remaining two sandwiches. Cut the sandwiches in half and serve.

IN SEASON NOW Apples are at their peak in the fall, but they're not the only ones. If you want to mix it up a little, try substituting pears for apples in this dish.

8 slices applewood
  smoked bacon
8 slices Brie
8 slices sourdough bread
2 Honeycrisp
  apples, peeled and
  thinly sliced
4 tablespoons honey
  or fig jam

Toasted Turkey Reubens

SERVES 4 | PREP TIME: 5 MIN | COOK TIME: 8 MIN

NUT-FREE

There is something so hard to resist about a grilled cheese sandwich. And this one is no exception. This one includes sliced turkey and sauerkraut to replicate the best flavors of a Rueben sandwich. Slather on the Thousand Island dressing and enjoy.

4 tablespoons Thousand Island dressing

8 slices rye bread

8 ounces deli smoked turkey breast

1 cup sauerkraut

8 slices Swiss cheese

2 tablespoons butter

1. Assemble the sandwiches by spreading 1 tablespoon salad dressing on 4 slices of the bread.

2. Top each with 2 ounces turkey, ¼ cup sauerkraut, 2 slices cheese, and the remaining slices of bread.

3. In a skillet over medium heat, melt the butter. Add two sandwiches to the skillet, cheese-side down, and cook until browned, 3 to 4 minutes. Flip the sandwiches and cook until browned and the cheese is melted, 3 to 4 minutes.

4. Repeat with the remaining two sandwiches. Cut the sandwiches in half and serve.

VARIATION The classic Reuben is made with corned beef. Our turkey version is a little healthier. It's fun to have both options on hand and let your guests choose which they prefer.

Tandoori Chicken Wraps

SERVES 4 | PREP TIME: 10 MIN | COOK TIME: 10 MIN

NUT-FREE

Tandoori chicken is traditionally made by marinating chicken in yogurt and spices and roasting it. In this recipe, the chicken is cooked with spices on the stovetop and served in a wrap topped with a sauce of yogurt and lemon juice. Like the classic dish, these Indian-inspired wraps are bursting with flavor, and they come together in mere minutes.

1. In a sauté pan over medium-high heat, combine the chicken, soy sauce, 1 tablespoon curry powder, and cayenne pepper. Cook thoroughly about 8 minutes.

2. In a small bowl, mix together the yogurt, remaining 2 teaspoons curry powder, and lemon juice and season with salt and pepper. Set sauce aside.

3. Divide the shredded cabbage, scallions, and cilantro evenly among the tortillas. Top with the chicken and drizzle with the sauce. Fold in the sides of the tortillas and roll them up. Cut in half and serve.

VARIATION Greek yogurt forms the base of this delicious sauce, but if you have sour cream, that will work fine as well.

2 pounds chicken tenders

2 tablespoons low-sodium soy sauce

1 tablespoon plus 2 teaspoons curry powder, divided

¼ teaspoon cayenne pepper

1 cup plain Greek yogurt

½ teaspoon lemon juice

Salt and black pepper

1½ cups shredded red cabbage

3 scallions, thinly sliced

2 tablespoons chopped fresh cilantro

6 (10-inch) flour tortillas

Sloppy Joes

SERVES 4 | PREP TIME: 8 MIN | COOK TIME: 2 TO 4 HOURS

DAIRY-FREE / GLUTEN-FREE / NUT-FREE / WORTH THE WAIT

This recipe is sure to bring back childhood memories. Rather than using the canned version, our homemade joes are nearly as quick and taste oh-so-much-better than their processed cousins.

1. Combine the turkey, salt and pepper, onion, bell pepper, garlic, ketchup, mustard, brown sugar, vinegar, and cayenne pepper in the slow cooker and stir well.

2. Cook on high for 2 hours or on low for 4 hours. Serve on potato rolls or with tortilla chips.

HELPFUL HINT Because you aren't browning the meat and draining it before you put it in the slow cooker, it's important you choose very lean ground beef so you don't have a puddle of grease in your slow cooker.

1 pound lean ground beef or turkey

Salt and black pepper

¼ onion, diced

½ green bell pepper, diced

3 garlic cloves, minced

1 cup ketchup

1 teaspoon mustard

1 tablespoon brown sugar

1 tablespoon red wine vinegar

¼ teaspoon cayenne pepper

Potato rolls or tortilla chips

Chipotle Bean Burritos

SERVES 4 | PREP TIME: 10 MIN | COOK TIME: 16 MIN

VEGETARIAN / NUT-FREE

I always keep the ingredients for burritos in my pantry and I suggest you do, too. Burritos are always a hit with every member of my family, and it's a big plus to be able to customize any toppings so everyone loves what they are eating.

1. In a large nonstick sauté pan over medium-high heat, warm the olive oil. Add the onion and cook until softened, 4 to 5 minutes. Add the garlic and cook for 30 seconds.

2. Add the black beans, chipotle powder, and water and bring to a boil. Reduce the heat to medium and simmer for 10 minutes.

3. Remove from the heat and stir in the salsa. Using a fork, partially mash the bean mixture. Season with salt and pepper to taste.

4. Wrap the tortillas in a paper towel and microwave for 45 seconds, until warm.

5. Divide the bean mixture equally between the tortillas. Top each with cheese, lettuce, sour cream, and additional salsa, if desired. Fold in the sides of the tortillas, roll them up, and serve.

HELPFUL HINT Warming the tortillas slightly makes them much easier to roll and improves their flavor.

1 tablespoon extra-virgin olive oil

½ onion, diced

2 garlic cloves, minced

2 (15.5-ounce) cans black beans, drained and rinsed

½ teaspoon chipotle powder

⅓ cup water

¼ cup salsa, plus more for serving (optional)

Salt and black pepper

6 (10-inch) flour tortillas

1 cup shredded Mexican blend cheese

1 head romaine lettuce, shredded

1 cup sour cream or plain Greek yogurt

Seared Brussels Sprouts with Bacon and Parmesan

SERVES 4 | PREP TIME: 6 MIN | COOK TIME: 15 MIN

GLUTEN-FREE / NUT-FREE

This is the recipe I make when someone says they don't like Brussels sprouts. The bacon and Parmesan perfectly complement this hidden gem of a vegetable, and I'm sure it will make a believer out of you.

1. In a large skillet over medium-high heat, cook the bacon until crispy. Transfer to a paper towel. When cool, crumble the bacon.

2. Add the Brussels sprouts and onion to the skillet, season lightly with salt and pepper and cook until tender, 5 to 8 minutes.

3. Turn off the heat, add the cheese and crumbled bacon, and stir to combine.

HELPFUL HINT Opt for fresh Brussels sprouts for this dish. Frozen sprouts will leach out too much water, making it virtually impossible for them to brown well.

5 strips bacon

1 pound Brussels sprouts, halved

1 onion, diced

Salt and black pepper

¼ cup shaved Parmigiano-Reggiano

Rosemary-Roasted Root Veggies

SERVES 4 | PREP TIME: 15 MIN | COOK TIME: 25 MIN

GLUTEN-FREE / VEGETARIAN / NUT-FREE

Whether enjoyed as a side or the main dish, this mélange of vegetables is super-satisfying. It's always a good idea to cook similar-size vegetables together, but carrots are denser than mushrooms and will take longer to roast. To prevent mushy or undercooked vegetables, I've devised a way to prepare them in two separate batches, using the same sheet pan, and then combine them after roasting.

1. Preheat the oven to 400°F and place the sheet pan inside the oven.

2. In a large bowl, toss the Brussels sprouts, cauliflower, and carrot with 2 tablespoons olive oil and season with salt and pepper. Spread the vegetables out on the sheet pan and roast for 12 to 15 minutes, stirring halfway through the baking time, until tender and browned in spots. Transfer to a plate and set aside.

3. In the bowl, toss the fennel, mushrooms, onion, and rosemary with the remaining 2 tablespoons olive oil and season with additional salt and pepper. Transfer the mixture to the sheet pan and roast for 8 to 10 minutes, until just softened.

4. Toss all the vegetables together. Season with salt and pepper to taste and garnish with Pecorino-Romano and a splash of balsamic vinegar. Serve immediately.

IN SEASON NOW This recipe makes the most of fall's veggies, but there are tons of others you might like to try, like broccoli, parsnips, and turnips. Experiment and find your favorite combination.

2 cups halved
  Brussels sprouts

2 cups cauliflower florets

2 cups baby carrots

4 tablespoons extra-virgin
  olive oil, divided

Salt and black pepper

1 bulb fennel, sliced

1 pound button or cremini
  mushrooms, quartered

1 red onion, sliced

2 sprigs rosemary

½ cup shaved
  Pecorino-Romano

2 tablespoons
  balsamic vinegar

Artichoke and Spinach Bake

SERVES 4 | PREP TIME: 15 MIN | COOK TIME: 45 MIN

VEGETARIAN / NUT-FREE

The roasted artichokes and spinach are wonderful in this casserole, but when mixed with the crispy bread, fontina, and Parmesan, it turns into a showstopper. Leftovers reheat well, so this is a good one to have for lunch the next day.

1. Preheat the oven to 375°F. Coat a 9-by-13-inch baking dish with cooking spray.

2. In a microwave-safe bowl, place the spinach and the water, cover, and microwave for 2 to 3 minutes. Cool slightly. Place the spinach in a clean kitchen towel and squeeze to remove any excess liquid.

3. In the same bowl, mix together the spinach, onion, artichoke hearts, bread, and fontina. Transfer the mixture to the baking dish and sprinkle with the Parmesan.

4. In a measuring cup, whisk together the milk, mustard, and egg, season with salt and pepper, and pour over the bread. Bake for 30 to 35 minutes or until set.

5. For a crispy top, place the baking pan under the broiler for 3 to 4 minutes or until the edges are lightly browned.

HELPFUL HINT This dish can be made 1 day ahead. Cover the baking dish and refrigerate until ready to bake.

Nonstick cooking spray, for greasing the dish

1 (8-ounce) bag fresh spinach

2 tablespoons water

½ onion, diced

1 (6.5-ounce) jar marinated artichoke hearts, drained and chopped

2 cups 1-inch cubed sourdough or ciabatta bread

1 cup shredded fontina

¼ cup grated Parmigiano-Reggiano

⅔ cup milk

½ teaspoon Dijon mustard

1 large egg

Salt and black pepper

Pan-Seared Cauliflower Steaks with Gruyère and Garlic

SERVES 4 | PREP TIME: 10 MIN | COOK TIME: 32 MIN

GLUTEN-FREE / VEGETARIAN / NUT-FREE

This dish stands on its own as a light vegetarian lunch or dinner, though it also serves as a great side dish alongside a perfectly cooked rib eye steak. Cauliflower, when roasted, becomes caramelized, giving it a surprising sweetness that is very appealing.

6 tablespoons
  butter, divided
1 head cauliflower, cut into
  1-inch steaks
Salt and black pepper
4 garlic cloves, minced
½ teaspoon red
  pepper flakes
½ cup grated Gruyère
1½ tablespoons
  lemon juice
1 tablespoon chopped
  fresh parsley

1. Preheat the oven to 400°F.

2. In an oven-safe skillet over medium-high heat, warm 2 tablespoons butter. Add two cauliflower steaks, season with salt and pepper, and cook until well browned on the bottom, about 5 minutes. Flip the cauliflower and cook until browned, about 5 minutes. Transfer to a plate and set aside. Repeat with the rest of the cauliflower.

3. Add the remaining 4 tablespoons butter to the pan, as well as the garlic and red pepper flakes. Working in batches, place the skillet in the oven and bake for 6 minutes or until the cauliflower is tender but not mushy.

4. Garnish with Gruyère, lemon juice, and parsley.

HELPFUL HINT The hardest part about this recipe is keeping the cauliflower from falling apart. Your best bet is to slice it a little thicker than you might think. One-inch slices seem to work the best. Use a wide spatula to flip the steaks and keep them intact.

Gnocchi with Brown Butter, Sage, and Parmesan

SERVES 4 | PREP TIME: 5 MIN | COOK TIME: 20 MIN

NUT-FREE

Gnocchi are typically cooked in water like pasta and then tossed in a sauce, but I prefer to roast them. I think it gives them a nicer flavor and texture. The pancetta and Parmigiano-Reggiano add savory saltiness and pair well with the sage.

1. Preheat the oven to 450°F.

2. In a 9-by-9-inch baking dish, mix together the gnocchi, pancetta, sage, and olive oil and season with salt and pepper. Roast for 12 to 15 minutes or until the gnocchi begins to brown.

3. Transfer the gnocchi to a bowl. Add the butter to the baking dish and bake just until the butter begins to brown, 5 to 6 minutes.

4. Toss the gnocchi in the brown butter to coat. Garnish with the cheese and serve.

VARIATION Gnocchi is traditionally made with potatoes, but you can now find them made with cauliflower and sweet potato. Additionally, if you can't find pancetta, you can always substitute bacon.

1 (16-ounce) bag frozen gnocchi

4 ounces pancetta, diced

¼ cup chopped fresh sage

3 tablespoons extra-virgin olive oil

Salt and black pepper

8 tablespoons butter

⅓ cup grated Parmigiano-Reggiano

Spaghetti and Meatballs

SERVES 4 | PREP TIME: 15 MIN | COOK TIME: 35 MIN

NUT-FREE

Spaghetti and meatballs is a classic, and this recipe will not disappoint. Just be sure to stir the spaghetti as soon as you put it into the pot of water to prevent it from sticking. Continue to do this often while it cooks.

1. Fill a Dutch oven two-thirds full with salted water and bring it to a boil. Add the spaghetti and cook until al dente, 8 to 9 minutes. Drain the pasta in a colander and set aside in a warm serving bowl.

2. In a large bowl, combine the sausage, ground beef, garlic powder, bread, milk, egg, and cheese and season with salt and pepper. Using a small ice cream scoop, form the mixture into meatballs.

3. In the Dutch oven, over medium-high heat, warm the olive oil. Add the meatballs and cook until browned, turning to cook all sides, 6 to 7 minutes. Work in batches if necessary so you don't crowd the pan.

4. Pour off any excess oil. Add the crushed tomatoes, garlic, oregano, and basil, stirring to combine. Bring to a boil and cook for 2 minutes. Reduce the heat to medium-low and simmer for 15 minutes. Season with additional salt and pepper to taste.

5. Serve the sauce and meatballs over the spaghetti.

IN SEASON NOW This recipe uses canned tomatoes, but if you had an overabundance of tomatoes from the summer that you canned, they would really raise the flavor bar on this sauce.

1 pound spaghetti

½ pound spicy
   Italian sausage

½ pound lean ground beef

2 teaspoons garlic powder

2 slices bread, torn
   into pieces

¼ cup milk

1 large egg, beaten

¼ cup grated
   Parmigiano-Reggiano

Salt and black pepper

2 tablespoons extra-virgin
   olive oil

1 (28-ounce) can crushed
   tomatoes

5 garlic cloves, minced

1 teaspoon dried oregano

¼ cup chopped fresh basil

Gourmet Four-Cheese Mac and Cheese

SERVES 4 | PREP TIME: 12 MIN | COOK TIME: 20 MIN

VEGETARIAN / NUT-FREE

Who doesn't love a great bowl of mac and cheese? And this recipe, with its four cheeses, is the ultimate in cheesy goodness. The decadent combination of sharp Cheddar, smoked Gouda, nutty Gruyère, and the ever-popular Parmigiano-Reggiano is an international celebration of cheese and pasta. Enjoy!

1. Fill a Dutch oven with salted water and bring to a boil over high heat. Add the pasta and cook until al dente, 12 to 14 minutes. Drain and set aside.

2. Reheat the Dutch oven over medium-high heat, melt the butter, whisk in the flour, and cook for 2 minutes.

3. Add the milk and cream and bring to a boil, whisking constantly until it thickens slightly, 2 to 3 minutes.

4. Whisk in the Cheddar, Gouda, Gruyère, and Parmesan until smooth.

5. Season with the paprika, cayenne, and salt and pepper and stir to combine. Add the pasta and stir until completely combined with the cheese sauce. Serve hot.

8 ounces penne

4 tablespoons butter

4 tablespoons all-purpose flour

2 cups whole milk

½ cup heavy cream

1 cup grated sharp Cheddar

½ cup grated smoked Gouda

¼ cup grated Gruyère

¼ cup grated Parmigiano-Reggiano

1 teaspoon smoked paprika

⅛ teaspoon cayenne pepper

Salt and black pepper

VARIATION I've called for my favorite cheeses here, but feel free to use whatever you prefer. Just be sure to use the largest amount of the cheese you want to be most prominent.

Pasta with Wild Mushroom and Gorgonzola Cream Sauce

SERVES 4 | PREP TIME: 10 MIN | COOK TIME: 18 MIN

VEGETARIAN / NUT-FREE

Mushroom lovers will really love this one. It's earthy with a decadent cream sauce that is so rich and silky. Pair it with a great pinot noir and invite over someone special. Use goat cheese instead of Gorgonzola if the flavor is too strong for you.

1. Bring a stockpot filled with salted water to a boil over high heat. Add the linguine and cook until al dente, about 9 minutes. Drain in a colander and set aside in a warm serving bowl.

2. In the same pot, melt the butter, add the mushrooms, and sauté until softened, 3 to 4 minutes. Add the garlic and cook for 30 seconds.

3. Pour in the heavy cream and whisk to combine. Reduce the heat to low, add the Pecorino-Romano and Gorgonzola, and whisk until combined.

4. Stir in the lemon juice, season with salt and pepper to taste, and serve over the linguine.

VARIATION If you can't find a variety of wild mushrooms, you can always use button or creminis. Additionally, if you prefer blue cheese to Gorgonzola, use that instead.

½ pound linguine

4 tablespoons butter

1 pound assorted mushrooms, thinly sliced (shiitake, oyster, and cremini)

4 garlic cloves, minced

¾ cup heavy cream

½ cup grated Pecorino-Romano

¼ cup crumbled Gorgonzola

1 tablespoon lemon juice

Salt and black pepper

Garlic Butter–Basted Salmon with Broccolini

SERVES 4 | PREP TIME: 8 MIN | COOK TIME: 15 MIN

GLUTEN-FREE / NUT-FREE

Need to get a healthy, delicious dinner on the table in minutes? Salmon with broccolini to the rescue. It's kid-friendly without making the adults feel like they're eating from the child's menu.

1. Preheat the oven to 375°F. Line a sheet pan with parchment paper.

2. Place the salmon on one side of the sheet pan and the broccolini on the other. Drizzle lightly with olive oil and season with salt and pepper. Roast for 8 to 10 minutes or until the fish is cooked through and the broccolini is tender.

3. In a small microwaveable bowl, combine the butter and garlic and microwave until the butter is melted. Stir to combine.

4. Pour the garlic butter over the salmon. Bake for 2 minutes.

5. Drizzle with lemon juice and serve.

VARIATION Salmon is both delicious and beautiful in this dish, but feel free to use whatever fish you have or prefer.

4 (6-ounce) salmon fillets

1 pound broccolini, trimmed

2 tablespoons extra-virgin olive oil

Salt and black pepper

8 tablespoons butter

4 garlic cloves, minced

1½ tablespoons lemon juice

Seafood Enchiladas

SERVES 4 | PREP TIME: 15 MIN | COOK TIME: 35 MIN

NUT-FREE

Love traditional enchiladas, but sometimes yearn for something a little lighter? Meet our seafood version—delicate shrimp and crab bask in a light cream sauce with just a touch of spice. I think you'll find it's a nice alternative to the classic.

1. Preheat the oven to 350°F. Place the butter in a 9-by-13-inch baking dish and place the pan in the oven until the butter is melted.

2. Add the shrimp, onion, and garlic to the baking dish and bake for 5 minutes or until the shrimp is cooked.

3. Transfer the shrimp mixture to a large bowl, add the crab and half of the cheese, as well as the sour cream and Old Bay. Mix well.

4. Divide the mixture equally between the tortillas. Roll them up and place them, seam-side down, in the baking dish.

5. In the large bowl, combine the heavy cream and salsa verde and pour it over the enchiladas.

6. Bake for 25 minutes. Top with the remaining half of the cheese. Bake for another 5 minutes.

7. Garnish with cilantro and serve.

VARIATION Scallops would be delicious in this dish as well. To make them easier to eat, opt for the smaller bay scallops.

1 tablespoon butter

½ pound shrimp (size 21/25), peeled, deveined, cut into 1-inch pieces

½ onion, finely diced

4 garlic cloves, minced

½ pound crabmeat

10 ounces shredded Monterey Jack, divided

½ cup sour cream

1 teaspoon Old Bay seasoning

6 (10-inch) flour tortillas

1 cup heavy cream

1 cup salsa verde

2 tablespoons chopped fresh cilantro

Shrimp Diane

SERVES 4 | PREP TIME: 10 MIN | COOK TIME: 12 MIN

GLUTEN-FREE / NUT-FREE

This is a variation of the dish made famous by Southern chef Paul Prudhomme. I've upped the quantities of herbs and backed off on the spice a bit, which I think appeals to a wider range of taste buds. This is an elegant meal worthy of entertaining and it's amazing served with your favorite artisan bread.

1. In a large bowl, toss together the shrimp, garlic, cayenne, basil, thyme, and oregano and season with salt and pepper.

2. In a large sauté pan over medium-high heat, melt 2 tablespoons butter. Add the shallot and mushrooms and sauté until they soften, 3 to 4 minutes. Add the shrimp and cook until they just turn pink, another 1 to 2 minutes. Add the wine and cook, stirring to deglaze the pan, until almost all of it evaporates.

3. Pour in the stock and bring to a boil. Reduce the heat to medium-low, add the remaining 6 tablespoons butter in pieces, and simmer, swirling the pan until the sauce is creamy.

4. Season with salt and pepper to taste. Garnish with parsley and serve.

VARIATION The star of this dish is typically the shrimp. But if you prefer scallops, they would be lovely as well.

1½ pounds (21/25) shrimp, peeled, deveined

3 garlic cloves, minced

¼ teaspoon cayenne

½ teaspoon dried basil

½ teaspoon dried thyme

¼ teaspoon dried oregano

Salt and black pepper

8 tablespoons butter, divided

1 shallot, diced

½ pound button mushrooms, sliced

¼ cup dry white wine

¼ cup seafood or low-sodium chicken stock

2 tablespoons chopped fresh parsley

Glazed Salmon with Couscous and Spinach

SERVES 4 | PREP TIME: 10 MIN | COOK TIME: 25 MIN

NUT-FREE

If you're in the mood for a light, fresh, but incredibly satisfying seafood meal, look no further than this orange and maple–glazed salmon. It has that sweet-savory combination that is beloved by so many, especially me!

1 cup water

1 tablespoon extra-virgin olive oil

½ teaspoon salt, plus more to taste

1 cup instant couscous

4 (6-ounce) salmon fillets

Black pepper

4 tablespoons butter

1 pound fresh baby spinach

½ cup orange juice

¼ cup maple syrup

2 teaspoons orange zest

1. In a sauté pan over high heat, bring the water to a boil with the olive oil and salt. Add the couscous, cover, turn off the heat, and let stand for 5 minutes. Using a fork, fluff the couscous, and transfer it in a bowl.

2. Season the salmon with salt and pepper.

3. In the same sauté pan melt the butter, add the salmon and sauté until they are nicely browned, 3 to 5 minutes. Flip the salmon and sauté until browned, 3 to 5 minutes.

4. Arrange the spinach in the pan alongside the salmon. Pour the orange juice and maple syrup over the salmon, cover, and cook until the spinach wilts, 3 minutes. Season with additional salt and pepper to taste.

5. Spoon the couscous into shallow bowls, top with spinach and salmon, and garnish with orange zest.

HELPFUL HINT There are a lot of different species of salmon to choose from and any will do in this recipe. King salmon, also known as Chinook salmon, is the most sought after because of its moderate-to-full flavor and high oil content.

Thai Chicken Curry

SERVES 4 | PREP TIME: 15 MIN | COOK TIME: 30 MIN

DAIRY-FREE / GLUTEN-FREE / NUT-FREE

Thai cuisine is so much easier to prepare than you might think. All you need are the right ingredients, like red curry paste and coconut milk, and a few minutes on the stove to release their intensely delicious flavors.

1. In a stockpot over medium-high heat, warm the olive oil. Add the curry paste and cook 1 minute.

2. Add the carrot, onion, and bell pepper and cook, stirring occasionally until the onion is softened and translucent, about 8 minutes.

3. Add the potatoes, chicken, coconut milk, water, curry powder and sriracha and bring to a boil. Reduce the heat to medium and simmer, stirring occasionally until the chicken is cooked through and the potatoes are tender, about 20 minutes. Season with salt and pepper to taste.

4. Divide the curry among four bowls and garnish with the basil and lime wedges.

VARIATION Want to make this a vegetarian main dish? Use chickpeas instead of the chicken. It will also greatly reduce your cook time, as the beans are already cooked.

1 tablespoon extra-virgin olive oil

4 ounces red curry paste

4 carrots, peeled, cut into slices

1 onion, diced

1 red bell pepper, diced

3 red potatoes, cubed

2 pounds chicken tenders, cut into 1-inch cubes

1 (15-ounce) can unsweetened coconut milk

1 cup water

2 tablespoons curry powder

1 tablespoon sriracha

Salt and black pepper

2 tablespoons thinly sliced fresh basil

1 lime, quartered

Buffalo Chicken Nachos

SERVES 4 | PREP TIME: 12 MIN | COOK TIME: 20 MIN

GLUTEN-FREE / NUT-FREE

Should we have nachos tonight? Or maybe we should have wings? Make this recipe and you can have the best of both worlds. Parchment paper is your best friend here, so there is practically no cleanup. If you like your nachos spicier, top with your favorite hot sauce.

1. Preheat the oven to 375°F. Line a sheet pan with parchment paper.

2. Place the chicken on the sheet pan and pour the oil and hot sauce over the top. Bake for 12 minutes, or until it is cooked through. Transfer the chicken to a plate.

3. Line the sheet pan with a new sheet of parchment paper. Spread the tortilla chips out on the pan and top with the cooked chicken.

4. In a separate bowl, mix together ¼ cup blue cheese crumbles and the mayonnaise, cream, garlic, and lemon juice and season with salt and pepper. Dot the chicken with the blue cheese mixture. Top with the diced celery, scallions, Cheddar, and the remaining ¼ cup blue cheese.

5. Bake for 8 to 10 minutes, until the cheese melts.

HELPFUL HINT Have some leftover chicken from another dinner? You're one step closer to making these delicious nachos. Simply shred the chicken and save yourself a step.

2 skinless, boneless chicken breasts, cut into strips

4 tablespoons extra-virgin olive oil

⅓ cup hot sauce

1 (16-ounce) bag tortilla chips

½ cup blue cheese, crumbled, divided

⅓ cup mayonnaise

¼ cup heavy cream, half-and-half, or milk

2 garlic cloves, minced

Juice of ½ lemon

Salt and black pepper

2 celery stalks, diced

3 scallions, thinly sliced

1 cup shredded Cheddar or Monterey Jack

Chicken with Creamy Corn and Bacon

SERVES 4 | PREP TIME: 20 MIN | COOK TIME: 35 MIN

GLUTEN-FREE / NUT-FREE

Here is a recipe that looks like an elegant dish, but it's really comfort food in disguise. The chicken is nicely browned and cooked with sweet corn and salty bacon in a seasoned cream sauce. Serve it for dinner on its own or as a main course for a dinner party.

1. In a Dutch oven over medium-high heat, cook the bacon until crispy, 8 to 10 minutes. Transfer to a paper towel. Crumble when cooled.

2. Remove all but 1 tablespoon of excess fat from the pan. Add the corn, onion, and garlic and sauté until lightly browned, 3 to 4 minutes. Transfer to a plate and set aside.

3. Season the chicken breasts with salt, pepper, and thyme (if using dried). Add the olive oil if there is no bacon fat left in the pan.

4. Add the chicken breasts and cook until they are well browned and an instant-read thermometer reads 165°F when inserted into the thickest part of the breast, about 15 minutes. Transfer to the plate with the corn mixture and set aside.

4 slices bacon

1 cup corn

½ onion, diced

2 garlic cloves, minced

4 skinless, boneless chicken breasts, pounded ½-inch thick

Salt and black pepper

1 teaspoon dried thyme or 2 sprigs fresh

1 tablespoon extra-virgin olive oil (optional)

1¼ cups heavy cream or half-and-half

½ cup grated Parmigiano-Reggiano

1 tablespoon lemon juice

5. Add the heavy cream, cheese, thyme (if using fresh), and lemon juice to the pan, whisk to combine, and bring a boil. Cook until the mixture thickens slightly, about 4 minutes.

6. Season with additional salt and pepper to taste. Place the chicken on plates and top with the corn mixture, bacon, and cream sauce.

HELPFUL HINT I've given you the option of using dried or fresh thyme in this dish. You'll notice that they appear at different times. That's because dried herbs need more time to let their flavors develop in a dish. Fresh herbs, on the other hand, will lose their delicate flavors if they spend too much time under heat, so add them near the end of the recipe.

Chicken Potpie

SERVES 4 | PREP TIME: 15 MIN | COOK TIME: 1 HOUR 10 MIN

NUT-FREE / WORTH THE WAIT

If there is one recipe you should have memorized, it's a chicken potpie. Universally loved, easy to make, and impressive to serve, this is a great choice for almost any situation. If you want a really beautiful presentation, make it in a cast-iron skillet and serve it straight from the oven to the table.

1. Preheat the oven to 400°F.

2. In an oven-safe skillet over high heat, combine the chicken stock, chicken, carrot, and potatoes and bring to a boil. Cook until the chicken is cooked through and the vegetables are tender, 8 to 10 minutes.

3. Transfer the contents of the skillet to a bowl and set aside.

4. In the same skillet over medium-high heat, melt the butter, add the onion, and sauté until soft, 4 to 5 minutes. Sprinkle in the flour and whisk for 2 minutes. Add the bowl of reserved chicken and vegetables and the half-and-half, whisking until smooth. Add the thyme, sherry, and peas. Season with salt and pepper to taste.

5. Top with the piecrust and brush with the beaten egg. Using a sharp knife, cut vents into the top.

6. Bake for 45 minutes, until bubbly and the crust is lightly browned.

HELPFUL HINT You can always make your own piecrust, but premade refrigerated doughs are nice to have on hand as a time-saver. Be sure to take it out of the refrigerator as you're starting to prep. This will give it time to warm up, making it easier to unroll without breaking.

1½ cups low-sodium chicken stock

2 skinless, boneless chicken breasts, cut into 1-inch cubes

2 large carrots, peeled and cut into slices

2 medium potatoes, peeled and diced

4 tablespoons butter

½ onion, diced

¼ cup all-purpose flour

⅔ cup half-and-half

1 teaspoon dried thyme

2 tablespoons dry sherry

½ cup peas

Salt and black pepper

1 refrigerated piecrust

1 large egg, beaten in 1 teaspoon water

Herb-Roasted Chicken

SERVES 4 | PREP TIME: 20 MIN | COOK TIME: 1 HOUR 15 MIN

GLUTEN-FREE / NUT-FREE / WORTH THE WAIT

There is almost nothing better than coming home to the aromas of a roasting chicken. With potatoes, carrots, and Brussels sprouts, this dish (as shown on the book's cover) is a very hearty one-dish meal.

1. Preheat the oven to 450°F.

2. Remove the bag of giblets from inside the chicken. Rinse the bird well with cold water, let drain, and pat dry. Truss the chicken with kitchen twine by tying the legs together and tucking the wings underneath.

3. In a small bowl, combine the butter, sage, thyme, and garlic and season with salt and pepper. Gently rub the mixture under the skin of the chicken and rub whatever is left on the outside of the bird. Place the chicken, potatoes, carrots, and Brussels sprouts in a 9-by-13-inch baking dish and roast for 15 minutes.

4. Lower the over temperature to 350°F and continue to roast for 1 hour, or until the internal temperature reaches 165°F in the thickest part of the thigh. Cover the bird loosely with aluminum foil and let rest for about 15 minutes before serving.

HELPFUL HINT To really get the most flavor and juiciness from your bird, flip it! That's right. About halfway through roasting it, turn it completely over to redistribute the juices. Just before taking it out of the oven, turn it right-side up. It will be perfectly roasted and delicious.

1 (5- to 7-pound) roasting chicken
3 tablespoons butter, softened
1 teaspoon dried sage
1 teaspoon dried thyme
2 garlic cloves, minced
Salt and black pepper
½ pound baby potatoes
½ pound baby carrots
½ pound Brussels sprouts

Chicken a la King

SERVES 4 | PREP TIME: 12 MIN | COOK TIME: 18 MIN

NUT-FREE

Here is a recipe that might seem old-fashioned, but the reason it's still around is because it tastes so good. My mom used to make this every so often (not enough in my opinion), and it's still one of my all-time favorites. I like it best served over toast.

1. Season the chicken with salt and pepper. In a large sauté pan over medium-high heat, melt 2 tablespoons butter. Add the chicken and cook until cooked through, 5 to 7 minutes.

2. Add the remaining 2 tablespoons butter and the mushrooms, then sauté until softened, 3 to 4 minutes.

3. In a measuring cup, whisk together the chicken stock, half-and-half, cornstarch, ground mustard, and cayenne and pour into the sauté pan, whisking until smooth. Bring to a boil and continue to whisk until the sauce thickens, 2 to 3 minutes.

4. Add the peas, sherry, and Worcestershire sauce and season with additional salt and pepper to taste.

HELPFUL HINT Don't forgo the sherry or the Worcestershire in this dish. They might just seem like frivolity at the end of the recipe, but their deep flavors and bite of acid really help to develop layers of flavor in a big way.

2 skinless, boneless chicken breasts, cut into 1-inch cubes

Salt and black pepper

4 tablespoons butter, divided

½ pound button or cremini mushrooms, sliced

1½ cups low-sodium chicken stock

1 cup half-and-half

¼ cup cornstarch

½ teaspoon ground mustard

Dash cayenne pepper

½ cup frozen peas

2 tablespoons sherry

1 teaspoon Worcestershire sauce

Chicken with Butternut Squash and Barley

SERVES 4 | PREP TIME: 15 MIN | COOK TIME: 2 TO 6 HOURS

DAIRY-FREE / NUT-FREE / WORTH THE WAIT

With its warm spices—ginger and cloves—this comforting dish is what to serve when you want to warm up a chilly autumn day. Head outside and take a walk, rake some leaves, or play with your kids, and come home to a heartwarming meal that really satisfies.

1. In a small bowl, mix together the ginger, cloves, cayenne, brown sugar, salt, and pepper. Rub the mixture over the chicken breasts.

2. Place the chicken breasts in a slow cooker along with the onion, garlic, butternut squash, barley, chicken stock, and orange juice. Cook on high for 2 to 3 hours or on low for 5 to 6 hours.

3. Season with additional salt and pepper to taste. Add the balsamic vinegar, stir to combine, and serve.

VARIATION The flavors used in this dish pair equally well with pork. A tenderloin or chops would work nicely in this recipe.

¼ teaspoon ground ginger

¼ teaspoon ground cloves

¼ teaspoon cayenne pepper

1 tablespoon brown sugar

½ teaspoon salt

½ teaspoon black pepper

4 skinless, boneless chicken breasts

¼ cup diced onion

3 garlic cloves, minced

1 butternut squash, cut into 1-inch cubes

1 cup barley

½ cup low-sodium chicken stock

¼ cup orange juice

1 tablespoon balsamic vinegar

Butter Chicken

SERVES 4 | PREP TIME: 15 MIN | COOK TIME: 15 MIN

GLUTEN-FREE / NUT-FREE

It's hard to believe you can coax such incredible flavor out of these ingredients in just five minutes. The pressure cooker will be very hot on sauté mode, so work quickly to prevent the vegetables and tomato paste from burning in the pot. Serve with warmed naan, and you'll have a dining table filled with happy eaters.

1. Preheat the pressure cooker on sauté.

2. Add the butter, onion, garlic, and ginger to the pot and cook for 2 minutes. Add the tomato paste, water, chicken, curry powder, smoked paprika, cumin, turmeric, cayenne, and sugar, season with salt and pepper, and stir to combine.

3. Close and lock the lid, closing off the vent, and pressure cook on high for 5 minutes. Allow the pressure cooker to depressurize naturally. Remove the lid and add the heavy cream, stirring to combine. Season with salt and pepper to taste.

ALT POT Try preparing this dish in your Dutch oven. Follow step 1, cover the pot, and let the chicken simmer in the liquid for 20 to 25 minutes or until tender. Finish with cream and season to taste.

3 tablespoons butter

½ large onion, diced

4 garlic cloves, minced

1 (1-inch) piece fresh ginger, grated

1 (6-ounce) can tomato paste

1 cup water

4 skinless, boneless chicken breasts, cut into 1-inch cubes

1 tablespoon curry powder

1 teaspoon smoked paprika

1 teaspoon ground cumin

½ teaspoon ground turmeric

¼ teaspoon cayenne pepper

1 tablespoon sugar

Salt and black pepper

¾ cup heavy cream

Pecan-Stuffed Pork Chops with Bourbon Gravy

SERVES 4 | PREP TIME: 20 MIN | COOK TIME: 40 MIN

You're going to feel like you've died and gone to Kentucky with this dish. The pecan stuffing and bourbon gravy will have you planning a road trip. A side salad would round out this meal.

1. Preheat the oven to 350°F.

2. In a Dutch oven over medium-high heat, add 2 tablespoons butter, the onion, and the celery and sauté until softened, 5 to 6 minutes.

3. Add the bread crumbs, pecans, and thyme, season with salt and pepper, and stir to combine. Transfer to a bowl and set aside.

4. Cut a slit horizontally in each of the pork chops deep enough to create a pocket. Divide the stuffing equally between each pork chop. Season the exterior of the pork chops with additional salt and pepper.

5. In the Dutch oven over medium-high heat, melt the remaining 3 tablespoons butter. Add the pork chops and cook until browned on both sides, 10 to 12 minutes. Transfer the chops to a plate and set aside.

5 tablespoons
butter, divided

½ onion, diced

2 celery stalks, diced

½ cup toasted
bread crumbs

¼ cup toasted
chopped pecans

1 teaspoon dried thyme

Salt and black pepper

4 (1½-inch-thick)
pork chops

2 tablespoons
all-purpose flour

1 cup low-sodium
chicken stock

½ cup half-and-half

2 tablespoons bourbon

6. Whisk the flour into the Dutch oven and cook for 5 minutes until browned. Add the chicken stock and cook, stirring to deglaze the pan.

7. Pour in the half-and-half and bourbon, return the pork chops to the pan, and bake for 15 minutes, until the chops are cooked through.

HELPFUL HINT Use a sharp paring knife to cut slits in the chops. Hold your hand flat on the top of the chop and cut with your other hand. It's also important that you don't cut too far back otherwise the stuffing will peek out the back of the chop.

Roasted Pork Tenderloin with Parsnips and Baby Carrots

SERVES 4 | PREP TIME: 10 MIN | COOK TIME: 40 MIN

DAIRY-FREE / GLUTEN-FREE / NUT-FREE

This dish screams "fall" with its roasted pork, parsnips, and carrots enveloped in a sweet and spicy maple-chipotle sauce. It's what we all love about autumn—warm meals on cool nights.

1. Preheat the oven to 400°F. Place a 9-by-13-inch baking dish inside the oven.

2. Season the tenderloin with salt and pepper and drizzle with olive oil.

3. Carefully place the pork in the hot baking dish and turn it to sear on all sides. Add the parsnips and carrots and roast for 25 minutes, or until the internal temperature of the pork reads 145°F. Transfer the pork and vegetables to a plate, cover, and let rest for 10 minutes.

4. Pour the chicken stock into the baking dish and, using a wooden spoon, scrape the browned bits off the bottom. Whisk in the maple syrup and chipotle peppers. Return the baking dish to the oven and bake for 5 minutes, or until heated through. Season with additional salt and pepper to taste and serve over the sliced pork.

HELPFUL HINT Pork tenderloins are perfect for a weeknight meal as they are smaller than the full loin and cook quickly. They typically come in packs of two, so feel free to roast both and freeze the second for another meal.

1 pound pork tenderloin

Salt and black pepper

2 tablespoons extra-virgin olive oil

2 parsnips, peeled and cut into 1-inch cubes

1 cup baby carrots

¼ cup low-sodium chicken stock

⅓ cup maple syrup

2 chipotle peppers in adobo sauce, minced

Adobo Pork with Rice

SERVES 4 | PREP TIME: 35 MIN | COOK TIME: 30 MIN

DAIRY-FREE / GLUTEN-FREE / NUT-FREE

This take on the famous Filipino-style meat is marinated in vinegar to give it that classic twang adobo is known for. It's a simple preparation that makes a wonderful companion for the rice.

1. In a metal bowl, mix together the vinegar, soy sauce, garlic, and bay leaf and season with salt and pepper. Add the pork chops and marinate for 30 minutes.

2. Remove the pork and reserve the marinade.

3. In a large sauté pan over medium-high heat, warm the oil. Add the pork and cook until browned, 4 minutes per side.

4. Add the rice and cook, stirring until lightly toasted.

5. Add the stock and reserved marinade and cook, stirring to deglaze the pan.

6. Bring to a boil and cook for 2 minutes. Reduce the heat to medium-low, cover, and simmer until the rice is tender, about 20 minutes. Remove the bay leaf and serve.

VARIATION This dish works equally well with chicken, if you prefer.

1 cup white vinegar

¼ cup low-sodium soy sauce

1 whole head garlic, peeled and crushed

1 bay leaf

Salt and black pepper

2 pounds boneless pork chops, thinly sliced

2 tablespoons extra-virgin olive oil

1 cup rice

1 cup low-sodium chicken stock

Jambalaya

SERVES 4 | PREP TIME: 15 MIN | COOK TIME: 25 MIN

GLUTEN-FREE / DAIRY-FREE / NUT-FREE

If you want to add shrimp to this dish, stir them in just after cooking is complete. Cover the pressure cooker, but don't lock it down. Let the shrimp cook in the hot jambalaya for 3 to 5 minutes. Either way, don't let the jambalaya sit in the pressure cooker once the cooking is complete or the rice will become mushy.

1. Preheat the pressure cooker on sauté. Rub the chicken with the Cajun seasoning.

2. Add the olive oil, chicken, and sausage to the pot and cook until browned, 6 to 8 minutes.

3. Add the onion, celery, and bell pepper and sauté until the vegetables are just tender, 5 to 7 minutes. Add the garlic and cook for 30 seconds.

4. Add the tomato sauce, diced tomatoes, chicken stock, and rice and stir to combine.

5. Close and lock the lid, closing off the vent, and pressure cook on high for 6 minutes. Quick release the pressure. Open the pot and season with salt and pepper to taste. Serve immediately.

ALT POT Jambalaya is easy to prepare in a sauté pan or Dutch oven with a lid. Follow the recipe through step 3, cover, lower the heat to medium and simmer for 20 minutes, or until the rice is cooked through.

4 skinless, boneless chicken breasts, cut into 2-inch pieces

1 tablespoon Cajun seasoning

2 tablespoons extra-virgin olive oil

½ pound andouille sausage, cut into slices

1 onion, diced

3 celery stalks, diced

1 green bell pepper, diced

4 garlic cloves, minced

½ cup tomato sauce

1 (14.5-ounce) can diced tomatoes

2½ cups low-sodium chicken stock

1½ cups rice (like Uncle Ben's converted)

Salt and black pepper

Carnitas

SERVES 4 | PREP TIME: 15 MIN | COOK TIME: 50 MIN

DAIRY-FREE / GLUTEN-FREE / NUT-FREE

This traditional Mexican dish literally means "little meat," probably because after it cooks, either in the pressure cooker as done here or for hours in a Dutch oven, it shreds into small pieces of deliciousness.

1. Preheat the pressure cooker on sauté. Season the pork with salt and pepper.

2. In a small bowl, combine the garlic, cumin, oregano, brown sugar, coriander, and smoked paprika and sprinkle the mixture over the pork to coat.

3. Add the olive oil to the pot, add the pork, and cook until browned, 5 to 6 minutes. Pour in the orange juice, lime juice, and water.

4. Close and lock the lid, closing off the vent, and pressure cook on high for 40 minutes. Allow it to depressurize on its own or carefully set it to quick release.

5. Season with additional salt and pepper to taste, then use two forks to shred the pork. Serve with corn tortillas, avocado slices, cilantro, and lime wedges.

ALT POT These pork carnitas are also wonderful cooked in a Dutch oven. After you have browned them and added the liquids, cover the pot and place it in a 350°F oven for 2 hours or until the pork is very tender and shreds easily.

4 pounds pork shoulder,
  cut into 2-inch cubes

Salt and black pepper

4 garlic cloves, minced

1 tablespoon ground cumin

1 tablespoon
  dried oregano

2 teaspoons light
  brown sugar

1 teaspoon ground
  coriander

1 teaspoon
  smoked paprika

2 tablespoons extra-virgin
  olive oil

Juice of 2 oranges

Juice of 1 lime plus 1 lime,
  cut into wedges

1 cup water

8 corn tortillas

Avocado slices

Chopped cilantro

Italian-Style Meat Loaf and Roasted Potatoes

SERVES 4 | PREP TIME: 8 MIN | COOK TIME: 50 MIN

NUT-FREE

This recipe is an Italian take on the classic American comfort food with the addition of oregano, basil, and mozzarella. Garlicky roasted potatoes balance this satisfying meal.

1. Preheat the oven to 350°F.

2. In a large bowl, mix together the marinara, ground beef, bread crumbs, onion, oregano, basil, egg, and mozzarella and season with salt and pepper. Do not overmix or the meatloaf will be tough. Place the mixture on one side of a 9-by-13-inch baking dish, shaping it until uniform in size.

3. Bake for 30 minutes. Place the potatoes on the other side of the baking dish, toss with the garlic and olive oil, and season with additional salt and pepper. Bake for another 20 minutes, or until the meatloaf registers 160°F on an instant-read thermometer. Let sit for 10 minutes before cutting into slices and serving.

VARIATION For a very traditional "gravy," mix together ⅓ cup ketchup and ¼ cup brown sugar and spread it over the top of the meatloaf. Place the baking dish back in the oven for 5 minutes.

⅓ cup marinara sauce

1½ pounds lean ground beef

½ cup Italian bread crumbs

½ onion, diced

1 teaspoon dried oregano

1 teaspoon dried basil

1 large egg

½ cup shredded mozzarella

Salt and black pepper

½ pound baby potatoes, quartered

2 garlic cloves, minced

1 tablespoon extra-virgin olive oil

Beef Stroganoff

SERVES 4 | PREP TIME: 15 MIN | COOK TIME: 30 MIN

NUT-FREE

Beef stroganoff is such a classic comfort food—meaty steak and earthy mushrooms enveloped in a rich cream sauce and served over egg noodles. It's perfect for those chilly autumn evenings after a long day at work.

1. In a Dutch oven filled with salted water, cook the egg noodles until al dente, 3 to 4 minutes. Drain and set aside on a warmed serving platter.

2. Season the steak with salt, pepper, and dill. Add the olive oil to the Dutch oven and warm over medium-high heat. Add the steak and cook until browned, 3 to 4 minutes.

3. Add the onion and mushrooms and cook until softened, 4 minutes. Add the garlic and cook for 30 seconds. Sprinkle the flour over the mixture and cook for 2 minutes.

4. Add the beef stock, Worcestershire sauce, and Dijon mustard, whisking and scraping the bottom of the pan to remove the browned bits, and bring to a boil.

5. Cook for 2 to 3 minutes or until the sauce thickens slightly. Reduce the heat to medium-low, cover, and simmer for 10 minutes. Stir in the sour cream, season with salt and pepper to taste, and serve over the egg noodles.

HELPFUL HINT Be sure to cut the steak nice and thin—not only will it cook more quickly, it will also tenderize the beef.

8 ounces egg noodles

1 pound sirloin steak, cut into ½-inch strips

Salt and black pepper

2 teaspoons dried dill

2 tablespoons extra-virgin olive oil

1 onion, diced

10 ounces cremini or button mushrooms, quartered

2 garlic cloves, minced

3 tablespoons all-purpose flour

2 cups low-sodium beef stock, divided

2 tablespoons Worcestershire sauce

1 tablespoon Dijon mustard

1 cup sour cream

Mongolian Beef

SERVES 4 | PREP TIME: 8 MIN | COOK TIME: 2 TO 5 HOURS

DAIRY-FREE / NUT-FREE / WORTH THE WAIT
Served in lettuce wraps or over leftover rice, this super-easy and incredibly flavorful beef is the perfect weeknight meal to come home to or to make on the weekends when you'd rather be outside than making dinner in the kitchen.

1. In a slow cooker, combine the steak, cornstarch, ginger, garlic, soy sauce, stock, brown sugar, red pepper flakes, and vinegar and cook on high for 2 to 3 hours or on low for 4 to 5 hours.

2. Season to taste, garnish with scallions, and serve.

HELPFUL HINT Cut the steak against the grain to be sure the meat is as tender as possible. When you cut with the grain, the meat will be very hard to chew.

1½ pounds flank or skirt steak, thinly sliced against the grain

⅓ cup cornstarch

1 tablespoon grated ginger

6 garlic cloves, minced

⅓ cup low-sodium soy sauce

⅓ cup beef stock

½ cup dark brown sugar

2 teaspoons red pepper flakes

1 tablespoon rice wine vinegar

4 scallions, chopped

Coffee-Rubbed Brisket with Sweet Potatoes

SERVES 4 | PREP TIME: 5 MIN | COOK TIME: 1 HOUR 25 MIN

DAIRY-FREE / GLUTEN-FREE / NUT-FREE / WORTH THE WAIT

What would normally take hours to roast in the oven is on the table in just over an hour. The coffee rub on this brisket is downright heavenly and is a nice contrast to the sweetness of the sweet potatoes.

1. Preheat the pressure cooker on sauté. In a small bowl, mix together the coffee, cinnamon, and cardamom and rub it over the brisket. Season the brisket with salt and pepper.

2. Add the olive oil and brisket to the pot and brown on both sides, 8 to 10 minutes.

3. Pour in the beef stock. Place the sweet potatoes in a metal bowl that fits in the pressure cooker and place it on top of the brisket.

4. Close and lock the lid, closing off the vent, and pressure cook on high for 1 hour 10 minutes.

5. Either allow the pressure cooker to depressurize naturally or carefully slide the quick release button. Transfer the brisket to a plate and cover to keep warm.

6. Mash the sweet potatoes in the metal bowl with the butter until smooth. Season to taste.

1 tablespoon finely ground coffee or espresso

1 tablespoon ground cinnamon

1 teaspoon ground cardamom

1 (3- to 4-pound) brisket

Salt and black pepper

2 tablespoons extra-virgin olive oil

½ cup low-sodium beef stock

3 sweet potatoes, peeled and quartered

2 tablespoons butter

3 tablespoons cornstarch

¼ cup water

7. In a measuring cup, whisk together the cornstarch and water until smooth. With the pressure cooker on sauté, add the cornstarch mixture and cook, whisking constantly, until the sauce thickens, 1 to 2 minutes.

8. Season with additional salt and pepper to taste and serve over the brisket along with the sweet potatoes.

ALT POT Instead of an electric pressure cooker, you can always make this recipe in a Dutch oven. After browning it well on both sides and pouring in the stock, cover the pot and place it in a 350°F oven for 2 hours or until the beef is very tender. Then pick up at step 7, making the slurry to thicken the sauce.

WINTER

When the temperatures begin to plummet and the storm fronts settle in, it's time for comfort food. During the cold months we yearn for such classics as the rich gravy of beef Bourguignon and the thickly melted Gruyère of French onion soup. These hearty dishes with slow-cooked flavors warm not just the body but the soul, bracing you for whatever the weather outside brings.

Spicy Sausage Queso Dip

SERVES 4 | PREP TIME: 10 MIN | COOK TIME: 15 MIN

GLUTEN-FREE / NUT-FREE

Need a snack for the Super Bowl that everyone loves? Why not whip up a quick batch of queso, serve it with a big bowl of tortilla chips, and watch it disappear before the game even starts.

1. In a large sauté pan over medium-high heat, add the sausage and cook until browned and cooked through, about 5 minutes.

2. Add the onion and cook until translucent, about 4 minutes. Add the garlic and cook for 30 seconds. Sprinkle in the cornstarch and cook, stirring, for 2 minutes.

3. Pour in the beer and cook, whisking, until the beer has almost evaporated. Pour in the heavy cream and whisk to combine.

4. Reduce the heat to low, add the Velveeta and pepper Jack, and whisk until melted.

5. Add in the salsa, season with salt and pepper, and stir.

VARIATION You can make this a vegetarian queso by simply omitting the sausage.

1 pound spicy sausage
1 onion, diced
4 garlic cloves, minced
2 tablespoons cornstarch
½ cup light beer
1 cup heavy cream
8 ounces Velveeta, cubed
8 ounces pepper Jack, shredded
1 cup salsa
Salt and black pepper

Cream of Broccoli and Smoked Gouda

SERVES 4 | PREP TIME: 10 MIN | COOK TIME: 15 MIN

GLUTEN-FREE / VEGETARIAN / NUT-FREE

Broccoli and cheese are a match made in heaven, but you already know that. The difference here is using smoked Gouda, which gives it an added dimension of flavor. Be sure to have some great bread on hand for dipping.

1. In a Dutch oven over medium-high heat, warm the olive oil. Add the onion and sauté until translucent, about 4 minutes. Add the garlic and cook for 30 seconds.

2. Add the vegetable broth and broccoli, cover, and cook until the broccoli is softened, about 8 minutes.

3. Reduce the heat to low and, using an immersion blender, puree the soup until smooth.

4. Add the cheese and whisk until melted. Season with salt and pepper to taste.

VARIATION This recipe uses smoked Gouda, but a sharp Cheddar is also wonderful. If you want to give it a little more elegance, add a splash of heavy cream just before serving.

1 tablespoon extra-virgin olive oil

1 medium onion, diced

2 garlic cloves, minced

4 cups vegetable broth

1½ pounds broccoli florets

1½ cup shredded smoked Gouda

Salt and black pepper

Easy Ramen with Shrimp

SERVES 4 | PREP TIME: 10 MIN | COOK TIME: 15 MIN

DAIRY-FREE / GLUTEN-FREE / NUT-FREE

Traditional ramen can take days to make and requires a lot of obscure ingredients. Here I considered all of the things people love about ramen (noodles and savory broth) and created a quick-and-easy version you can make at home in no time.

1. In a stockpot over medium-high heat, bring the chicken stock, garlic, ginger, and soy sauce to a boil and cook for 5 minutes.

2. Add the noodles, mushrooms, shrimp, carrot, snow peas, and chili sauce and cook until the shrimp are done, about 3 minutes.

3. Turn off the heat and season with salt and pepper to taste.

4. Divide among four bowls, and garnish each with half an egg and a sprinkle of sesame seeds.

VARIATION If you prefer, chicken or tofu strips can easily replace the shrimp in this dish. If you're using chicken, just be sure to cook it a bit longer.

1 quart low-sodium chicken stock

3 garlic cloves, minced

1 (1-inch) piece ginger, grated

3 tablespoons low-sodium soy sauce

2 (3-ounce) packages ramen noodles

1 cup quartered cremini or button mushrooms

½ pound shrimp (size 21/25), peeled and deveined

1 carrot, cut into matchsticks

6 ounces (1½ cups) snow peas

1 tablespoon chili-garlic sauce

Salt and black pepper

2 hard-boiled eggs, peeled and cut in half

1 tablespoon sesame seeds

Hearty French Bean and Chicken Stew

SERVES 6 | PREP TIME: 15 MIN | COOK TIME: 1 HOUR

DAIRY-FREE / GLUTEN-FREE / NUT-FREE

This is actually is a weeknight version of the French classic, cassoulet. Serve it with a side salad and bread.

1. Preheat the oven to 350°F.

2. Rinse and dry the chicken well. Season with salt and pepper.

3. In a Dutch oven over medium heat, add the bacon and cook until crispy. Transfer the bacon to a plate and set aside.

4. Raise the heat to medium-high, add the chicken and sear, skin-side down, in the bacon fat until browned on all sides, about 12 minutes. Transfer the chicken to the plate with the bacon.

5. Add the onion, celery, and carrot and sauté until soft, about 5 minutes. Add the garlic and cook for 30 seconds.

6. Add the wine and cook, stirring to deglaze the pan, until the liquid is reduced by half, about 5 minutes. Add the beans, bay leaf, and thyme and stir to combine. Return the chicken and bacon to the pot.

7. Add the chicken stock and tomatoes, cover, and bake for 30 minutes. Remove the bay leaf and serve hot.

HELPFUL HINT Chicken thighs are so much more flavorful than breasts, so be sure to use them in this recipe. And if you get the bone-in thighs, they're even better.

6 bone-in, skin-on chicken thighs

Salt and black pepper

½ pound bacon, roughly diced

1 large onion, chopped

4 celery stalks, chopped

3 carrots, chopped

4 garlic cloves, minced

¾ cup dry white wine

2 (15.5-ounce) cans white beans, drained and rinsed

1 bay leaf

3 teaspoons dried thyme

2 cups chicken stock

1 (14.5-ounce) can diced tomatoes, drained

Smoked Turkey and Wild Rice Soup

SERVES 4 | PREP TIME: 10 MIN | COOK TIME: 25 MIN

GLUTEN-FREE / NUT-FREE

On a stormy day, few things are more satisfying than a creamy bowl of hot soup. When you combine wild rice and smoked turkey, you have a recipe for success, and you won't care that the weather outside is frightful.

1. In a stockpot over medium-high heat, melt the butter.

2. Add the onion and carrot and sauté until the onion is softened, about 4 minutes. Add the garlic and cook for 30 seconds.

3. Add the rice and stir to coat with the butter.

4. Add the chicken stock and stir well. Cover and cook until the rice is tender, about 20 minutes.

5. Add the milk, smoked turkey, sherry, and sage and season with salt and pepper.

HELPFUL HINT When you're grocery shopping, look for wild rice with a "quick-cook" label on the package.

1 tablespoon butter

½ onion, finely diced

1 large carrot, peeled and diced

2 garlic cloves, minced

¾ cup quick-cook wild rice

4 cups low-sodium chicken stock

1½ cups whole milk

½ cup diced smoked turkey

1 tablespoon sherry or other dry cooking wine

1 teaspoon fresh sage or fresh savory

Salt and black pepper

Cheeseburger Soup

SERVES 4 | PREP TIME: 15 MIN | COOK TIME: 25 MIN

NUT-FREE

Everything about this bowl of soup says "comfort food" with its creamy, meaty goodness. If you have young kids (or are just young at heart), this will quickly become a family favorite.

1. In a stockpot over medium-high heat, add the ground beef and cook until browned, 6 to 8 minutes. Drain and transfer to a bowl.

2. Add the beef stock, potatoes, onion, jalapeño, and garlic and bring to a boil. Lower the heat to medium, cover, and simmer until the potatoes are tender, about 8 minutes.

3. Add the ground beef and 2 cups milk and cook until heated through, 5 minutes.

4. In a measuring cup, combine the remaining ½ cup milk and the flour to make a smooth slurry.

5. Pour the slurry into the soup and bring to a boil, whisking constantly, until it thickens, about 2 minutes.

6. Add the Velveeta and cayenne and whisk until melted. Season with salt and pepper to taste and serve.

1 pound ground beef

1 quart low-sodium beef stock

2 large potatoes, peeled and diced

1 medium onion, diced

1 jalapeño, seeded and minced

1 garlic clove, minced

2½ cups milk, divided

3 tablespoons all-purpose flour

8 ounces Velveeta, cubed

¼ teaspoon cayenne pepper

Salt and black pepper

VARIATION You can make this soup as spicy as you like. Keep in mind that all of the heat in a jalapeño pepper is in the seeds and ribs. If you want a spicier soup, add all of those. If you want a milder soup, leave them out and just use the green part of the pepper.

Spicy Sausage and Kale Soup

SERVES 4 | PREP TIME: 10 MIN | COOK TIME: 25 MIN

GLUTEN-FREE / NUT-FREE

This easy-to-prepare soup is a riff on a popular Italian restaurant chain's version. Serve it with a crusty loaf of bread for dipping and you have a complete meal.

1. In a Dutch oven over medium-high heat, add the sausage and cook until it is browned, about 8 minutes. Drain off any excess fat, leaving 1 tablespoon in the stockpot. Transfer the sausage to a bowl and set aside.

2. Add the onion to the Dutch oven and cook until translucent, about 4 minutes. Add the garlic and cook for 30 seconds.

3. Lower the heat to medium, add the diced potatoes and stock and cook until the potatoes are fork-tender, about 8 to 10 minutes.

4. Add the sausage back to the pot along with the kale and heavy cream and stir until the kale is wilted. Season with salt and pepper to taste and serve.

IN SEASON NOW Kale is at its peak of flavor in the winter months, but if you don't like it you can always use spinach instead. It does cook much faster, so watch carefully to make sure you don't overcook it.

1 pound spicy sausage

1 large onion, diced

2 garlic cloves, minced

3 large potatoes, diced

4 cups low-sodium chicken stock

1 (8-ounce) bag fresh baby kale

½ cup heavy cream

Salt and black pepper

Black-Eyed Pea Soup

SERVES 4 | PREP TIME: 10 MIN | COOK TIME: 25 MIN

DAIRY-FREE / GLUTEN-FREE / NUT-FREE

In many parts of the country, most notably the South, eating black-eyed peas is an absolute must on New Year's Day. They are reputed to bring good luck, and who couldn't use a bit of that? Ham is the secret ingredient that brings all the flavors together.

1. Preheat the pressure cooker on sauté.

2. Pour the oil into the pot and heat until warmed. Add the onion and sauté until translucent, about 4 minutes. Add the garlic and cook for 30 seconds.

3. Add the ham bone, beans, broth, bay leaf, and thyme.

4. Close and lock the lid, closing off the vent, and pressure cook on high for 10 minutes.

5. Allow the pot to depressurize naturally.

6. Remove the lid, stir, and season with salt and pepper to taste. Remove the bay leaf before serving.

ALT POT Black-Eyed Pea Soup is also wonderful prepared in a Dutch oven or slow cooker. Add the ingredients to the Dutch oven, cover, and cook for about 30 minutes. If you prefer to try it in a slow cooker, cook on low for 8 hours or on high for 4 hours.

1 tablespoon extra-virgin olive oil

½ onion, diced

2 garlic cloves, minced

1 ham hock or ham bone

1 pound black-eyed peas, soaked overnight, drained, and rinsed

6 cups low-sodium vegetable broth or chicken stock

1 bay leaf

2 teaspoons dried thyme

Salt and black pepper

White Bean and Tomato Chili

SERVES 6 | PREP TIME: 10 MIN | COOK TIME: 25 MIN

DAIRY-FREE / NUT-FREE / VEGETARIAN

Do you know someone who thinks vegetarian soups aren't filling? This one will make them a convert. Cook extra. You're going to want it for later.

1. Preheat a pressure cooker on sauté.

2. Pour in the olive oil, then add the onion and celery and cook, stirring constantly, until they have softened, about 5 minutes. Add the garlic and cook for 30 seconds.

3. Add the white beans, chickpeas, paprika, cumin, salt, pepper, tomatoes, tomato paste, bulgur, and broth and stir to combine.

4. Close and lock the lid, closing off the vent, and pressure cook on high for 15 minutes.

5. Allow the pot to depressurize naturally or quick release the pressure.

6. Stir the soup and serve.

ALT POT You'll be amazed at how quickly and deliciously this comes together in the pressure cooker, but it can also easily be done in a stockpot, Dutch oven, or slow cooker. Just know it will take an extra 20 minutes or more.

1 tablespoon extra-virgin olive oil

½ large onion, diced

2 celery stalks, diced

3 garlic cloves, minced

2 (15.5-ounce) cans white beans, drained and rinsed

1 (15.5-ounce) can chickpeas, drained and rinsed

1 tablespoon smoked paprika

1½ teaspoons ground cumin

1½ teaspoons salt

1 teaspoon black pepper

1 (14-ounce) can diced tomatoes

2 tablespoons tomato paste

¼ cup bulgur wheat or couscous

3 cups vegetable broth

White Chicken Chili

SERVES 4 | PREP TIME: 5 MIN | COOK TIME: 4 TO 8 HOURS

**DAIRY-FREE / GLUTEN-FREE / NUT-FREE /
WORTH THE WAIT**

*If you want to dress things up a little more before
serving, set out sour cream, avocado slices, cilantro,
lime wedges, Monterey Jack cheese, and tortilla
chips, so everyone can personalize their bowl.*

1. In a slow cooker, mix together the stock,
   chicken, white beans, onion, green chiles, jalapeño, garlic, oregano, cumin, and coriander.

2. Cook on high for 4 hours or on low for 7 to
   8 hours.

3. Using two forks, shred the chicken.

4. Season with salt and pepper and serve.

HELPFUL HINT For the health-conscious, rest assured
knowing that rinsing the beans before adding them to the
pot eliminates about a quarter of the added sodium from
the beans.

2½ cups low-sodium
chicken stock

4 skinless, boneless
chicken breasts

2 (15.5-ounce) cans white
beans, drained and rinsed

1 large onion, diced

1 (4-ounce) can
green chiles

1 jalapeño, seeded and
finely diced

4 garlic cloves, minced

1½ teaspoons
dried oregano

1½ teaspoons
ground cumin

½ teaspoon ground
coriander

Salt and black pepper

Italian Seafood Stew

SERVES 4 | PREP TIME: 15 MIN | COOK TIME: 20 MIN

GLUTEN-FREE / NUT-FREE

Cioppino is a tomato-based soup featuring a multi-tude of seafood. Feel free to use whatever you prefer and leave out what you don't. Whatever you do, serve it with a great loaf of hearty bread to soak up all of those delicious juices.

1. In a stockpot over medium-high heat, melt the butter.

2. Add the onion and sauté until softened, about 4 minutes. Add the garlic, bay leaf, thyme, oregano, and red pepper flakes to the pot and cook for 30 seconds.

3. Add the wine, stirring to deglaze the pan, until nearly evaporated.

4. Add the tomatoes, chicken stock, and tomato paste and stir well. Add the clams, cover, and let cook 4 minutes.

5. Add the mussels and cook for an additional 3 minutes.

6. Add the shrimp and cod, cover, and cook for 2 minutes.

7. The stew is done when the clams and mussels have opened. Discard any unopened clams or mussels. Remove the bay leaf before serving.

VARIATION If you don't like cod or have another white fish on hand, feel free to use that instead.

2 tablespoons butter

1 onion, diced

4 garlic cloves, minced

1 bay leaf

1 teaspoon dried thyme

1 teaspoon dried oregano

1½ teaspoons red pepper flakes

½ cup dry white wine

1 (14.5-ounce) can diced tomatoes

1½ cups low-sodium chicken stock

2 tablespoons tomato paste

20 clams and mussels, divided

½ pound shrimp (size 21/25), peeled and deveined

1 (1½-pound) cod fillet

Winter Vegetable Beef Soup

SERVES 4 | PREP TIME: 15 MIN | COOK TIME: 25 MIN

DAIRY-FREE / NUT-FREE

This is a version of the soup my grandmother used to make. Not only is it delicious, but it's also a great memory-maker to share with family.

1. In a large stockpot over medium-high heat, warm the olive oil. Add the beef and cook until it is nicely browned, about 10 minutes.

2. Add the onion and cook until softened, about 4 minutes. Add the beef stock, cabbage, potatoes, frozen vegetables, tomatoes, and shell pasta and stir to combine.

3. Cook until the pasta is al dente, about 9 minutes. Season with salt and pepper to taste.

VARIATION If you want to go vegetarian with this soup, simply eliminate the beef and move right to step 2.

1 tablespoon extra-virgin olive oil

1 pound chuck roast, cut into bite-size pieces

1 onion, diced

2 cups beef stock or water

½ head cabbage, thinly sliced

3 potatoes, diced

1 (12-ounce) bag frozen mixed vegetables

2 (16-ounce) cans diced tomatoes

1 cup shell pasta

Salt and black pepper

Savory Beef Stew

SERVES 4 | PREP TIME: 10 MIN | COOK TIME: 1 HOUR 15 MIN

DAIRY-FREE / NUT-FREE / WORTH THE WAIT

If you love the flavor and aroma of slow-cooked dinners but don't have all day to prepare them, give this recipe a try. It's to die for on its own, but you should try it over leftover mashed potatoes. You won't regret it.

1. Preheat the oven to 350°F.

2. In a Dutch oven over medium-high heat, warm the olive oil. Add the beef and cook until browned, being careful not to crowd the pan, about 10 minutes.

3. Add the beef stock, garlic, lemon juice, tomato sauce, bay leaves, and onion and stir to combine. Cover and bake for 45 minutes.

4. Add the carrots, cover, and cook for an additional 30 minutes. Remove from the oven.

5. In a measuring cup, combine the flour and water and whisk until it forms a smooth slurry. Add the slurry to the pot and whisk until the sauces thickens.

6. Season with salt and pepper to taste, remove the bay leaves, and serve.

1 tablespoon extra-virgin olive oil

1¼ pounds cubed beef chuck roast

1¾ cups low-sodium beef stock

2 garlic cloves, minced

2 tablespoons lemon juice

1 (8-ounce) can tomato sauce

2 bay leaves

1 onion, diced

2 cups baby carrots

¼ cup all-purpose flour

½ cup water

Salt and black pepper

HELPFUL HINT Pat the beef dry with paper towels before cooking to ensure a lovely browned exterior.

Moroccan Beef Stew

SERVES 4 | PREP TIME: 15 MIN | COOK TIME: 1 HOUR 10 MIN

DAIRY-FREE / GLUTEN-FREE / WORTH-THE WAIT

Like a tagine, this dish uses ras el hanout: a blend of ground ginger, coriander, cinnamon, turmeric, nutmeg, allspice, and clove. Find it at your grocery or online—or you can always make your own. The stew is delicious served with warm flatbread to take advantage of all of the juices.

1. Preheat the oven to 400°F.

2. Toss the beef with the ras el hanout to coat.

3. In a Dutch oven over medium-high heat, warm the olive oil. Add the beef and cook until browned, about 10 minutes. It does not need to cook all the way through.

4. Add the onion, carrot, beef stock, and prunes, cover, and bake for 1 hour.

5. In a small bowl, combine the cornstarch and water to make a slurry. Add the mixture to the pot and whisk until the sauce thickens.

6. Season with salt and pepper to taste, garnish with the sliced almonds, and serve.

HELPFUL HINT Save yourself some extra prep time by having your butcher cut the chuck into cubes for you.

1½ pounds chuck roast, cut into 2-inch cubes

2 teaspoons ras el hanout

1 tablespoon extra-virgin olive oil

1 large onion, diced

2 large carrots, peeled and sliced

3 cups low-sodium beef stock

1½ cups prunes, roughly chopped

1 tablespoon cornstarch

1 tablespoon water

Salt and black pepper

¼ cup toasted sliced almonds

Apricot and Lamb Stew

SERVES 4 | PREP TIME: 10 MIN | COOK TIME: 2 HOURS

DAIRY-FREE / GLUTEN-FREE / WORTH THE WAIT

Lamb has a natural sweetness to it, and when you combine it with dried apricots and the warm spices of ras el hanout, you have a dish that is out of this world. Honestly, you will love it.

1. Season the lamb with the ras el hanout. In a Dutch oven over medium-high heat, warm the olive oil.

2. Add the lamb and sear until browned, 6 minutes on each side.

3. Move the lamb to one side of the Dutch oven, add the onion and the cinnamon stick, and cook until the onion softens, about 4 minutes. Add the garlic and cook for 30 seconds.

4. Reduce the heat to medium, add the chicken stock, cover, and simmer for 1 hour.

5. Add the carrot and apricots, cover, and cook for 30 minutes.

6. Add the honey, bring to a boil, and let the liquid reduce to a sauce-like consistency, about 6 minutes.

7. Season with salt and pepper to taste, garnish with the almonds and parsley, and serve.

VARIATION Lamb is absolutely delicious in this recipe, but it would work equally well with pork.

2 pounds lamb shoulder, cut into 2-inch cubes

1 tablespoon ras el hanout

1 tablespoon extra-virgin olive oil

1 large onion, diced

1 cinnamon stick

4 garlic cloves, minced

2 cups low-sodium chicken stock

3 carrots, cut into ¼-inch slices

1 cup chopped dried apricots

¼ cup honey

Salt and black pepper

¼ cup sliced almonds

2 tablespoons minced fresh parsley

French Onion Soup

SERVES 4 | PREP TIME: 15 MIN | COOK TIME: 35 MIN

VEGETARIAN / NUT-FREE

Yes, this classic dish is mostly made up of onions (cut them root to stem so they'll hold their shape) and broth, but you'll be amazed at how cooking onions for long enough makes them taste incredibly good. But let's be honest: It's really all about the cheese, so don't skimp when it comes to that last step.

1. Preheat the pressure cooker on sauté.

2. Add the butter to the pot and heat until melted. Add the onion and ½ teaspoon salt and cook for 20 minutes, stirring constantly. The bottom will be coated a deep brown.

3. Add the beer and cook, stirring to deglaze the pot. Add the stock, thyme, bay leaves, and Worcestershire and stir to combine.

4. Close and lock the lid, closing off the vent, and pressure cook on high for 10 minutes.

5. Allow the pot to depressurize naturally or quick release the pressure.

6. Season with additional salt and pepper. Remove the bay leaves.

7. Ladle the soup into bowls and top each with two slices of baguette. Sprinkle with the cheese and serve.

ALT POT This soup is also wonderful made in a Dutch oven. Follow the same steps up to the point of locking down the pressure cooker. Instead, simply let the soup continue to simmer for 20 minutes before you season it and top it with bread and cheese.

1 tablespoon butter

1½ pounds yellow onions, thinly sliced

Salt and black pepper

1 (12-ounce) lager beer

3 cups low-sodium beef stock

1 teaspoon dried thyme

2 bay leaves

1 tablespoon Worcestershire sauce

1 baguette, sliced into ½-inch-thick slices and toasted

8 ounces Gruyère, shredded

Roasted Halloumi Pitas

SERVES 2 | PREP TIME: 5 MIN | COOK TIME: 4 MIN

VEGETARIAN / NUT-FREE

Halloumi cheese is interesting because you can bake it and it won't melt. Thanks to peppery harissa (available in the international section of the supermarket), this handheld meal is great for when you are on the go and combines smoky flavor with the appealing slight bitterness of arugula.

1. Place an oven rack in the closest position to the broiler element. Set the oven to broil.

2. Wrap the pitas in aluminum foil and place in a lower position in the oven to warm.

3. Place the Halloumi on the sheet pan and drizzle with olive oil. Sprinkle with garlic and season with salt and pepper.

4. Broil until the cheese is slightly browned and beginning to melt, about 4 minutes.

5. Place one piece of cheese inside each of the pitas. Stuff each with baby arugula, balsamic vinegar, and harissa. Serve immediately.

VARIATION Can't find Halloumi? Try substituting bread cheese or a farmer's cheese. You want something that won't melt immediately or break apart.

2 large pitas, halved

7 ounces Halloumi cheese, halved

1 tablespoon extra-virgin olive oil

2 garlic cloves, minced

Salt and black pepper

1½ cups fresh baby arugula

½ teaspoon balsamic vinegar

2 tablespoons harissa

Pulled Pork Sandwiches

SERVES 4 | PREP TIME: 2 MIN | COOK TIME: 8 HOURS

DAIRY-FREE / NUT-FREE / WORTH THE WAIT

I love walking into the house greeted by the smell of slow-cooked pulled pork. It's inviting, and the best part is that making it is ridiculously easy. Just keep that to yourself though, and bask in the glory you'll get after you serve it to your family and friends.

1. In a slow cooker, add the pork chops and season with salt and pepper.

2. Add half of the barbecue sauce, cover and cook on high for 8 hours, stirring the chops every 2 hours.

3. The pork is done when it breaks apart easily with a fork.

4. Add the rest of the barbecue sauce, mix well, and shred the pork. Spoon into slider buns and serve.

VARIATION Skinless, boneless chicken breasts can easily substitute for pork chops if you prefer.

3 pounds boneless
  pork chops
Salt and black pepper
1 (28-ounce) bottle
  barbecue sauce
6 to 8 slider buns

Smoked Gouda, Mushroom, and Onion Grilled Cheese

SERVES 2 | PREP TIME: 4 MIN | COOK TIME: 15 MIN

VEGETARIAN / NUT-FREE

If you grew up loving grilled cheese as a kid, you're going to flip for this one. It's a gourmet, grown-up version with smoked Gouda and ciabatta that you've been waiting for your whole life.

1. In a sauté pan over medium-high heat, melt 1½ tablespoons butter. Add the onion and sauté until soft and translucent, about 4 minutes.

2. Add the mushrooms, season with salt and pepper, and cook until soft, about 4 minutes. Transfer the onion and mushrooms to a bowl.

3. Reduce the heat to medium. Place two slices of the bread in the sauté pan. Top each with two slices of cheese, some of the mushroom-onion mixture, and two more slices of cheese.

4. Spread the remaining ½ tablespoon butter on the remaining bread slices. Top the sandwiches with the bread, butter-side up. Cover and cook until browned and the cheese is melted, 5 to 6 minutes.

5. Flip the sandwiches and cook until browned, about 5 minutes.

HELPFUL HINT Be sure to place cheese on both sides of the filling. This will help the sandwich hold together when you flip it.

2 tablespoons
  butter, divided
1 yellow onion, thinly sliced
4 ounces cremini or button
  mushrooms, thinly sliced
Salt and black pepper
4 slices ciabatta or
  sourdough
8 thin slices smoked Gouda

Roasted Spaghetti Squash with Parmesan and Cherry Tomatoes

SERVES 4 | PREP TIME: 10 MIN | COOK TIME: 50 MIN

VEGETARIAN / NUT-FREE

This dish is delicious all on its own, but if you want to beef it up a bit, consider adding roasted chicken or even shrimp to the meal. Spaghetti squash is a wonderful vegetable that creates pasta-like strands and can stand in for traditional spaghetti.

1. Preheat the oven to 375°F.

2. Cut the squash in half lengthwise, then scoop out the seeds and discard. Place the squash in a 9-by-13-inch baking dish, and drizzle with 1 tablespoon olive oil and salt and pepper. Bake for 30 minutes.

3. Add the tomatoes, the remaining ½ tablespoon olive oil, and season with salt and pepper.

4. Bake for 20 minutes or until the squash easily pulls away from the outer skin. Place the squash on a work surface.

5. Using a fork, shred the spaghetti squash into strands. Transfer the squash strands to the baking dish with the tomatoes.

6. Add the butter, cheese, and lemon juice and stir to combine. Season with additional salt and pepper. Garnish with parsley and serve.

IN SEASON NOW Winter squash, such as the spaghetti squash used in this recipe, can be difficult to cut through. Use a sharp knife and a towel if necessary to stabilize it on your cutting board so it doesn't slip.

1 (4-pound) spaghetti squash
1½ tablespoons extra-virgin olive oil, divided
Salt and black pepper
½ pint cherry tomatoes
2 tablespoons butter
1 cup grated Parmigiano-Reggiano
1 tablespoon lemon juice
1 tablespoon chopped fresh parsley

Mushrooms with Farro Risotto

SERVES 4 | PREP TIME: 10 MIN | COOK TIME: 50 MIN

NUT-FREE / VEGETARIAN

Arborio rice is a short-grain rice traditionally used in risottos, but in this modern twist I use farro—a nutty grain that has a tender, chewy bite that has the same appeal and is perfect for chilly nights.

1. In a sauté pan over medium-high heat, melt 1 tablespoon butter. Add the mushrooms and sauté until soft, about 4 minutes.

2. Add the garlic and farro and stir to coat well with the butter.

3. Add the wine and cook, stirring to deglaze the pan, until it nearly evaporates.

4. Reduce the heat to medium and add ½ cup vegetable broth, stirring constantly until the liquid is absorbed.

5. Continue to add broth, ½ cup at a time, until all of the broth has been incorporated and the farro is al dente, about 45 minutes.

6. Stir in the cheeses, cut the remaining 1 tablespoon butter into small pieces, and add it to the risotto.

7. Season with salt and pepper to taste and serve.

HELPFUL HINT When cleaning mushrooms, don't immerse them in water. They'll absorb too much water and become soggy. Instead, reach for a damp paper towel and lightly dust off any dirt.

2 tablespoons butter, divided

8 ounces shiitake, oyster, or cremini mushrooms, thinly sliced

4 garlic cloves, minced

1 cup farro

1 cup dry white wine

4 cups low-sodium vegetable broth, divided

½ cup grated Parmigiano-Reggiano

½ cup grated Gruyère

Salt and black pepper

Garlic-Roasted Shrimp with Baby Potatoes

SERVES 4 | PREP TIME: 10 MIN | COOK TIME: 18 MIN

GLUTEN-FREE / NUT-FREE

Shrimp is a great choice for weeknight cooking because it cooks so quickly. It's become one of my favorite proteins. Keep a bag in the freezer for nights you just can't bear to cook (or if you just love shrimp like I do).

1 pound baby potatoes, quartered

6 tablespoons extra-virgin olive oil, divided

Salt and black pepper

1½ pounds (21/25) shrimp, shell-on

4 tablespoons butter, melted

6 garlic cloves, minced

½ teaspoon red pepper flakes

2 tablespoons minced fresh parsley

1. Preheat the oven to 400°F. Line a sheet pan with parchment paper.

2. Place the potatoes on the sheet pan, toss with 2 tablespoons olive oil, and season with salt and pepper.

3. Roast until the potatoes are fork-tender, about 10 minutes. Transfer the potatoes to a bowl and set aside.

4. Place an oven rack in the closest position to the broiler. Set the oven to broil.

5. Place the shrimp on the sheet pan. Add the melted butter, remaining 4 tablespoons olive oil, garlic, and red pepper flakes and toss well to coat.

6. Broil until the shrimp is opaque and the shells begin to brown, 2 to 4 minutes. Flip the shrimp and broil for 2 to 4 more minutes.

7. Garnish with the parsley and serve with the roasted potatoes.

ALT POT Rather than roasting the shrimp, you could also sauté them in a pan or skillet for 2 to 3 minutes.

Mediterranean Baked Cod

SERVES 4 | PREP TIME: 10 MIN | COOK TIME: 25 MIN

DAIRY-FREE / GLUTEN-FREE / NUT-FREE

This dish will have you feeling like you're dining along the Amalfi Coast. Good-quality canned tomatoes and frozen fish—if you can't get fresh—make this a great dinner when you are ultra-busy and don't have much time. Serve it over leftover rice or with a great bread if you like, but it's equally good all by itself.

1. Preheat the oven to 375°F.

2. In a 9-by-13-inch baking dish, stir together the crushed tomatoes, onion, garlic, eggplant, capers, paprika, and Italian seasoning. Season with salt and pepper.

3. Arrange the fish on top of the sauce and drizzle with the olive oil. Season with additional salt and pepper. Bake for 25 minutes or until the fish is just cooked through.

4. Drizzle with lemon juice and serve.

VARIATION You can substitute any fish you like. Just keep in mind that milder white fish like and flounder and tilapia are preferable, as they pair well with tomatoes.

1 (28-ounce) can crushed tomatoes

1 onion, diced

4 garlic cloves, minced

1 medium eggplant, peeled and diced

2 tablespoons capers, drained and rinsed

1 teaspoon smoked paprika

1 tablespoon Italian seasoning

Salt and black pepper

4 (6-ounce) cod fillets

1 tablespoon extra-virgin olive oil

1 tablespoon lemon juice

Sole with Brown Butter and Lemon

SERVES 4 | PREP TIME: 5 MIN | COOK TIME: 15 MIN

NUT-FREE

I've used a classic French preparation called meu-niere, *which just means the fillet has been dredged in flour before it hits the pan. This is one of the quickest, easiest and tastiest fish dishes you'll ever make.*

1. On a plate, combine the flour, salt, and pepper.

2. Lightly coat the fish fillets in the flour mixture, shaking off any excess.

3. In a skillet over medium-high heat, warm 2 tablespoons butter. Gently place the fish in the butter, being careful not to crowd the pan. You may need to cook them in two batches. Cook until the fillets are browned, about 3 minutes. Gently flip the fish and cook until browned, another 3 minutes.

4. Transfer the fish to a plate and loosely cover with aluminum foil to keep warm.

5. Add 2 tablespoons butter to the pan and add the broccolini. Cook until tender, 5 to 6 minutes.

6. Reduce the heat to medium, add the remaining 4 tablespoons butter to the pan and swirl until melted. Add the lemon juice and parsley and season with salt and pepper. Spoon the sauce over the fish and serve.

VARIATION We used sole in this dish, the classic choice. But feel free to use any fish you like. If you opt for a steak as opposed to a fillet, remember you will need to increase the cook time by 3 minutes.

½ cup all-purpose flour

1 teaspoon salt, plus more for seasoning

1 teaspoon black pepper, plus more for seasoning

6 (4-ounce) sole fillets

8 tablespoons butter, divided

1 pound broccolini, trimmed

2 tablespoons lemon juice

1 teaspoon chopped fresh parsley

Blackened Tuna with Mango Salsa

SERVES 4 | PREP TIME: 20 MIN | COOK TIME: 6 MIN

DAIRY-FREE / GLUTEN-FREE / NUT-FREE

This easy dinner is ideal for long, dark days when you need to imagine yourself somewhere warm and sunny. The sweetness and acidity of the mango salsa will surely brighten things up. Serve with tortillas.

1. In a bowl mix together the mango, red onion, jalapeño, lime juice, and cilantro. Season with salt and pepper and set aside.

2. In a small bowl, mix together the paprika, cumin, garlic powder, oregano, thyme, cayenne pepper, and ¼ teaspoon salt. Coat each tuna steak with the mixture.

3. In a sauté pan over high heat, warm the oil. Add the tuna and cook until seared, about 3 minutes on each side.

4. Serve with the mango salsa.

VARIATION Any type of fish can be used to make this dish. Thicker fish steaks, such salmon and mahi mahi, are a little easier to flip, but use whatever cut and variety you like to eat.

1 mango, diced

1 tablespoon minced red onion

½ small jalapeño, finely diced

1 tablespoon lime juice

2 teaspoons chopped fresh cilantro

¼ teaspoon salt, plus more for seasoning

Black pepper

2 teaspoons paprika

1½ teaspoons ground cumin

¾ teaspoon garlic powder

½ teaspoon dried oregano

¼ teaspoon dried thyme

¼ teaspoon cayenne pepper

4 (6-ounce) tuna steaks

2 tablespoons olive oil

Sheet-Pan Stir-Fry with Chicken and Veggies

SERVES 4 | PREP TIME: 10 MIN | COOK TIME: 15 MIN

DAIRY-FREE / NUT-FREE

Stir-fries are traditionally made in a wok or skillet, but this take on the classic dish is done on a sheet pan, making it much easier to clean up, plus you don't need to be constantly stirring. Serve it as-is or over rice. And don't forget the chopsticks.

1. Preheat the oven to 400°F. Line a sheet pan with parchment paper.

2. Place the chicken, carrot, bell pepper, and broccoli on the sheet pan. Season with salt and pepper and roast for 10 minutes.

3. In a measuring cup, mix together the soy sauce, oyster sauce, brown sugar, ginger, garlic, sesame oil, and cornstarch.

4. Add the snow peas to the sheet pan. Pour the sauce over the chicken and vegetables, stirring to coat everything.

5. Roast for 5 more minutes and serve.

IN SEASON NOW Winter can be a challenge when it comes to produce, but this recipe makes use of great veggies you can find all year long—broccoli, carrots, and snow peas.

2 pounds chicken tenders, cut into 2-inch pieces

2 carrots, thinly sliced

1 yellow bell pepper, diced

2 cups broccoli florets

Salt and black pepper

¼ cup low-sodium soy sauce

2 tablespoons oyster sauce

1 tablespoon brown sugar

1 (1-inch) piece ginger, grated

2 garlic cloves, minced

1 teaspoon sesame oil

1 teaspoon cornstarch

4 ounces (1 cup) snow peas

Moroccan-Spiced Chicken Wings

SERVES 4 | PREP TIME: 5 MIN | COOK TIME: 20 MIN

GLUTEN-FREE / NUT-FREE

Wings are good any time of the year, but they're especially tasty on game days. Double up the recipe and watch your fellow sports fans devour them.

1. Preheat the oven to 400°F. Line a sheet pan with parchment paper.

2. Place the chicken wings on the sheet pan.

3. In a bowl, mix together the butter, lemon juice, coriander, oregano, cumin, turmeric, cayenne pepper, black pepper, and salt. Pour the mixture over the chicken wings and toss to coat.

4. Roast for 10 minutes. Turn the chicken over and roast another 10 minutes.

5. Toss the chicken in the sauce in the pan and serve garnished with cilantro.

HELPFUL HINT Want to make a quick-and-easy dipping sauce to go with these wings? Add lemon juice and a little hot sauce to Greek yogurt.

2 pounds chicken wings

4 tablespoons butter, melted

1½ tablespoons lemon juice

2 teaspoons ground coriander

2 teaspoons dried oregano

1 teaspoon ground cumin

½ teaspoon ground turmeric

¼ teaspoon cayenne pepper

½ teaspoon black pepper

1 teaspoon salt

2 tablespoons chopped fresh cilantro

Chicken, Spinach, and Wild Rice Casserole

SERVES 4 | PREP TIME: 6 MIN | COOK TIME: 30 MIN

GLUTEN-FREE / NUT-FREE

The very best one-pot meals include meat, greens, and starch, and this one really delivers. Did I mention that it's delicious, too? The curry brings a surprise flavor that takes it over the top.

1. Preheat the oven to 350°F.

2. Place the rice, chicken, and mushrooms into a 9-by-13-inch baking dish.

3. Add the water and milk, stirring well to combine. Top with the bits of butter.

4. Cover the dish tightly with aluminum foil and bake for 20 minutes.

5. Add the spinach and sherry, cover, and continue to bake for another 10 minutes, until the rice is cooked.

6. Add the sour cream and the curry powder, season with salt and pepper, stir to combine, and serve.

HELPFUL HINT Be sure to get the quick-cook rice or you can even opt for precooked rice. If you go with the quick cook, make sure you cover the dish so the rice has a chance to steam and cook all the way through.

1 (6-ounce) package quick-cook wild rice

2 pounds chicken tenders, cut into bite-size cubes

8 ounces cremini or button mushrooms, thinly sliced

1½ cups water

½ cup whole milk

1 tablespoon butter, cut into small pieces

1 (10-ounce) bag fresh spinach

1 tablespoon sherry or other dry cooking wine

1 cup sour cream

1 tablespoon curry powder

Salt and black pepper

Easy Middle Eastern Chicken

SERVES 6 | PREP TIME: 12 MIN | COOK TIME: 15 MIN

DAIRY-FREE / NUT-FREE

Often referred to as "chicken shawarma," a traditional presentation is to wrap this chicken up with pita into a cone shape. The aromatic cumin, paprika, and cloves will transport you overseas, at least for a little while.

1. In a large bowl, mix together the cumin, turmeric, coriander, garlic powder, paprika, cloves, cayenne, and salt and pepper to taste. Add the chicken and toss to coat.

2. Add the onion, lemon juice, and olive oil and toss everything together.

3. Heat a sauté pan over medium-high and sauté the chicken mixture until the chicken is cooked through and the onion has softened, 12 to 15 minutes.

4. Serve in pitas or flatbreads.

HELPFUL HINT This dish is amazing with tzatziki sauce—an easy-to-make combination of Greek yogurt and diced cucumber with a bit of dill, parsley, and lemon juice.

1 tablespoon ground cumin

1 tablespoon ground turmeric

1 tablespoon ground coriander

1 tablespoon garlic powder

1 tablespoon smoked paprika

½ teaspoon ground cloves

½ teaspoon cayenne pepper

Salt and black pepper

3 pounds chicken tenders

1 large onion, thinly sliced

2 tablespoons lemon juice

⅓ cup extra-virgin olive oil

6 pitas or flatbreads

Dijon Chicken with Mushrooms and Almonds

SERVES 4 | PREP TIME: 10 MIN | COOK TIME: 15 MIN

GLUTEN-FREE

Craving something a little luxurious tonight? This pan-seared chicken in a mushroom-Dijon cream sauce is just the thing. It's rich, luscious, and cooks quickly for those in need of instant gratification. Serve alongside a mixed green salad.

1. In a sauté pan over medium-high heat, warm the olive oil.

2. Add the chicken breasts, being careful not to crowd the pan, and season with salt and pepper. Sauté until the chicken is golden brown, about 5 minutes. Flip and sauté until the other side is browned, another 5 minutes.

3. Add the mushrooms and shallot and cook until softened, about 4 minutes. Add the garlic and cook for 30 seconds.

4. Add the wine and cook, stirring to deglaze the pan, until the wine is reduced and the pan is nearly dry.

5. Add the heavy cream and mustard and whisk to combine.

6. Season with additional salt and pepper, garnish with toasted almonds and parsley, and serve.

HELPFUL HINT It's important to pound the chicken until it's ¼ inch thick, so it cooks quickly in the sauté pan. If it's too thick, it will burn on the outside before it fully cooks on the inside.

2 tablespoons extra-virgin olive oil

4 skinless, boneless chicken breasts, pounded thin

Salt and black pepper

8 ounces sliced button or cremini mushrooms

1 shallot, finely diced

4 garlic cloves, minced

½ cup dry white wine

1 cup heavy cream

2 teaspoons Dijon mustard

¼ cup toasted sliced almonds

1 tablespoon chopped fresh parsley

Kung Pao Chicken

SERVES 4 | PREP TIME: 10 MIN | COOK TIME: 15 MIN

DAIRY-FREE

This take-out favorite is just as great when you make it in your own kitchen. Adjust the red pepper flakes to appeal to your own level of spiciness. Serve it alone or over leftover grains or rice for the ultimate casual dinner.

1. In a measuring cup, mix together the chicken stock, soy sauce, sherry, hoisin, sugar, and cornstarch.

2. In a large skillet over medium-high heat, warm the oil. Add the chicken and cook until browned and cooked through, about 6 to 8 minutes.

3. Add the red bell pepper and cook until it is slightly softened, about 3 minutes. Add the garlic, ginger, and red pepper flakes and toss to combine.

4. Add the sauce and bring to a boil. Cook until it is a saucy consistency, about 4 minutes.

5. Season with salt and pepper and garnish with peanuts.

HELPFUL HINT Be sure to stir the sauce again before adding it to the pan, as the cornstarch has a tendency to sink to the bottom of the cup and become sludgy.

½ cup low-sodium chicken stock

1 tablespoon low-sodium soy sauce

4 tablespoons sherry or other dry cooking wine

1 tablespoon hoisin sauce

1 tablespoon sugar

1 tablespoon cornstarch

1 tablespoon vegetable oil

2 pounds chicken tenders, cut into 2-inch pieces

1 red bell pepper, diced

4 garlic cloves, minced

1 (1-inch) piece ginger, grated

1 teaspoon red pepper flakes

Salt and black pepper

½ cup peanuts

Cranberry-Glazed Pork Tenderloin with Roasted Potatoes and Green Beans

SERVES 4 | PREP TIME: 10 MIN | COOK TIME: 30 MIN

DAIRY-FREE / GLUTEN-FREE / NUT-FREE

Craving those Thanksgiving flavors? Give this recipe a try. The cranberry sauce, cinnamon, and orange will fill you with nostalgia.

1. Preheat the oven to 375°F. Line a sheet pan with parchment paper.

2. Place the pork on one side of the sheet pan. Arrange the potatoes and green beans on the other side of the pan.

3. Drizzle everything with the olive oil, season with salt and pepper, and roast for 20 minutes.

4. In a small bowl, mix together the orange juice, cornstarch, cinnamon, orange zest, brandy, and cranberry sauce.

5. Pour the sauce over the pork and bake for another 5 minutes, until the pork has reached an internal temperature of 145°F. Let rest for 10 minutes before cutting into slices and serving.

2 (1-pound) pork tenderloins

1 pound baby potatoes, quartered

1 pound green beans

2 tablespoons extra-virgin olive oil

Salt and black pepper

¼ cup orange juice

2 teaspoons cornstarch

¼ teaspoon ground cinnamon

Zest of ½ orange

2 tablespoons brandy or port

1 (16-ounce) can whole cranberry sauce

IN SEASON NOW Winter is the time of year when cranberries are at their peak. If you prefer to use fresh cranberries in this dish, make sure you add them to the pork as it is roasting.

Maple-Roasted Pork Loin

SERVES 4 | PREP TIME: 12 MIN | COOK TIME: 45 MIN

DAIRY-FREE / GLUTEN-FREE / NUT-FREE

The array of spices in this roasted pork dish are the perfect thing to warm you up, while the interplay of sweet and spicy in the sauce hits all the right notes.

1. Preheat the oven to 375°F. In a small bowl, mix together 1 teaspoon salt, the thyme, nutmeg, cinnamon, cardamom, and pepper and rub evenly over the pork.

2. In a Dutch oven over medium-high heat, warm 1 tablespoon olive oil. Add the pork, drizzle it with the remaining 1 tablespoon olive oil, and sear until it is browned on all sides, about 10 minutes total.

3. Place the sweet potato wedges in the pan with the pork and toss to coat in the oil. Cover and bake for about 15 minutes or until the internal temperature of the pork reads 145°F.

4. Transfer the pork and potatoes to a cutting board; cover loosely with aluminum foil.

5. Raise the heat to high, add the chicken stock to the Dutch oven, and cook, stirring to deglaze the pan, until the sauce is reduced by one-third.

6. Add the maple syrup and adobo sauce and whisk to combine. Cook for about 3 minutes until the sauces thickens slightly. Add the balsamic vinegar and season with additional salt and pepper. Cut the pork into slices and serve with the sauce.

HELPFUL HINT If you want to get dinner on the table quickly, be sure to get pork tenderloins. Smaller than the whole loin, they will cook much faster.

1 teaspoon salt, plus more for seasoning

½ teaspoon dried thyme

⅛ teaspoon ground nutmeg

¼ teaspoon ground cinnamon

⅛ teaspoon ground cardamom

½ teaspoon black pepper

2 tablespoons extra-virgin olive oil

2 (1-pound) pork tenderloins

2 sweet potatoes, each peeled and cut into 8 wedges

½ cup low-sodium chicken stock

½ cup maple syrup

1 tablespoon adobo sauce or 1 tablespoon smoked paprika

1 tablespoon balsamic vinegar

Potato, Spinach, and Ham Casserole

SERVES 6 | PREP TIME: 15 MIN | COOK TIME: 30 MIN

GLUTEN-FREE / NUT-FREE

It's difficult to believe that something so tasty can be made so easily and in just one baking dish. Prep is easy and minimal. This is the kind of go-to recipe that your friends and family will ask you to make, and only you will know how simple it is.

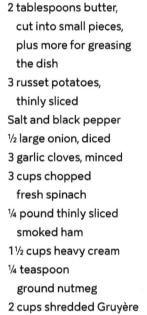

1. Preheat the oven to 400°F.

2. Generously butter a 9-by-13-inch baking dish. Place a layer of potatoes in the dish, covering the entire surface. Season with salt and pepper.

3. Add layers of onion, garlic, spinach, and ham. Finish with another layer of potatoes.

4. Pour the heavy cream over the dish, dot with butter, and season with nutmeg and additional salt and pepper.

5. Sprinkle the top with the cheese.

6. Bake for 25 to 30 minutes, or until the potatoes are fork-tender. Serve hot.

HELPFUL HINT It's really important that you slice the potatoes very thinly (a mandoline helps if you're not strong on knife skills). If they are too thick, the casserole will take much longer to cook.

2 tablespoons butter, cut into small pieces, plus more for greasing the dish

3 russet potatoes, thinly sliced

Salt and black pepper

½ large onion, diced

3 garlic cloves, minced

3 cups chopped fresh spinach

¼ pound thinly sliced smoked ham

1½ cups heavy cream

¼ teaspoon ground nutmeg

2 cups shredded Gruyère

Baked Ravioli with Sausage and Spinach

SERVES 6 | PREP TIME: 10 MIN | COOK TIME: 40 MIN

I really like this hearty pasta because it makes great use of quality prepared ingredients like artichoke hearts, bagged fresh spinach, and frozen ravioli. The flavor hits all the right notes with its combination of cheese, pasta, cream sauce, and Italian sausage. Think of it as all your favorite things rolled into one.

1. Preheat the oven to 350°F.

2. In a large oven-safe skillet over medium-high heat, cook the sausage until browned, about 6 minutes. Transfer to a plate and set aside. Pour off any excess fat.

3. Add the butter and garlic and sauté for 30 seconds. Pour in the heavy cream and whisk to incorporate.

4. Reduce the heat to low, add the grated cheese, and whisk until smooth. Season with salt and pepper. Pour two-thirds of the sauce into a measuring cup.

5. In a medium bowl, combine the spinach, artichoke hearts, pesto, and the cooked sausage. Pour half of the spinach mixture on top of the sauce in the skillet, spreading it out evenly.

6. Place half of the ravioli on top of the spinach followed by half of the remaining cream sauce.

7. Layer the remaining half of the spinach mixture, the rest of the ravioli and, finally, the rest of cream sauce.

8. Top with the mozzarella and bake for 30 minutes. Serve hot.

VARIATION If you don't want to mess with the spinach, you can substitute spinach ravioli for the cheese ravioli.

1 pound Italian sausage

4 tablespoons butter

1 garlic clove, minced

1 cup heavy cream

2 cups grated Parmigiano-Reggiano

Salt and black pepper

1 (4-ounce) bag fresh spinach, roughly chopped

1 (14-ounce) jar artichoke hearts, drained and chopped

¼ cup pesto

1 (25-ounce) bag frozen cheese ravioli

1½ cups shredded mozzarella

Southwest Casserole

SERVES 4 | PREP TIME: 10 MIN | COOK TIME: 4 HOURS 30 MIN

GLUTEN-FREE / NUT-FREE / WORTH THE WAIT

This super-simple weeknight dish also makes a great make-ahead meal. It keeps in the fridge for up to 3 days, but better yet, you can freeze it for a reheat-and-eat dinner in the future.

1. In a slow cooker, mix together the tomatoes, chicken stock, rice, chorizo, onion, cumin, chili powder, and paprika.

2. Cook on high for 4 hours, stirring occasionally.

3. Add the bell pepper and cook for another 30 minutes or until the rice is tender.

4. Season with salt and pepper, top with the pepper Jack, and serve.

HELPFUL HINT Be sure to use a long-grain rice, such as standard white or basmati. A short grain will produce too creamy of a texture for this dish.

1 (14.5-ounce) can diced tomatoes

1 cup low-sodium chicken stock

½ cup rice

1½ pounds chorizo sausage, cut into slices

1 onion, diced

1 teaspoon ground cumin

1 teaspoon chili powder

½ teaspoon smoked paprika

1 green bell pepper, diced

Salt and black pepper

1 cup shredded pepper Jack

Roast Lamb with Rosemary, Garlic, and Lemon

SERVES 4 | PREP TIME: 5 MIN | COOK TIME: 4 TO 8 HOURS

DAIRY-FREE / GLUTEN-FREE / NUT-FREE / WORTH THE WAIT

The sweet smell of lamb that has been cooking for hours is one of the most enticing aromas. This dish takes just minutes to assemble, but you'll be dreaming about it all day long. (If you want to leave this to cook all day while you're at work, set it to low and cook for about 8 hours.)

1. In a slow cooker, combine the lamb roast, onion, potatoes, and carrot. Pour in the red wine.

2. Cut small slits in the top of the lamb and insert the garlic cloves.

3. Lightly drizzle the olive oil over the top of the lamb and season with salt and pepper.

4. Cook on high for 4 hours or on low for 8 hours.

5. Add the rosemary sprigs and cook for 1 more hour or until the meat is very tender.

6. Garnish with lemon zest and serve.

2 pounds boneless lamb roast

1 large onion, diced

8 baby potatoes, quartered

1 cup baby carrots

½ cup dry red wine

4 garlic cloves

1 tablespoon extra-virgin olive oil

Salt and black pepper

2 sprigs fresh rosemary

Zest of ½ lemon

IN SEASON NOW This recipe calls for potatoes and carrots, but did you know that there are a wide variety of each, from purple to yellow? Explore the wide world of winter produce.

Beef and Broccoli Stir-Fry

SERVES 4 | PREP TIME: 12 MIN | COOK TIME: 14 MIN

DAIRY-FREE / NUT-FREE

There is a reason that beef and broccoli is a Chinese restaurant staple: It's absolutely delicious and very easy to prepare. Make this recipe and delight in a classic main dish.

1. Preheat the oven to 400°F. Line a sheet pan with parchment paper.

2. Combine the steak, broccoli florets, onion slices, 2 tablespoons soy sauce, 1 tablespoon brown sugar, black pepper, and red pepper flakes on the sheet pan and toss well to coat.

3. Roast for 10 minutes or until the broccoli is tender.

4. In a small bowl, mix together the remaining 2 tablespoons soy sauce, 2 tablespoons brown sugar, sesame oil, garlic, and ginger.

5. Pour the dressing over the beef and broccoli mixture and toss to combine. Roast for 1 minute.

6. Garnish with toasted sesame seeds and serve.

VARIATION If you really prefer not to use beef, then chicken, pork, or even tofu make a great substitute. If you do opt for chicken, you might need to extend the cooking time a bit to ensure it's thoroughly cooked.

2 (1½ pound) rib eye steaks, cut against the grain into ¼-inch-thick slices

1 head broccoli, cut into florets

1 onion, thinly sliced

4 tablespoons low-sodium soy sauce, divided

3 tablespoons brown sugar, divided

Black pepper

½ teaspoon red pepper flakes

1 tablespoon sesame oil

4 garlic cloves, minced

1 (1-inch) piece ginger, finely diced

1 teaspoon toasted sesame seeds

Korean-Style Barbecue

SERVES 4 | PREP TIME: 10 MIN | COOK TIME: 4 MIN

DAIRY-FREE / NUT-FREE

Also known as bulgogi, *this steak dish packs a ton of flavor into only 30 minutes of marinating. Cut the meat up early in the day before you head out, and you can give it a chance to marinate and soak even longer in all of those fabulous flavors. When you get home, dinner literally comes together in minutes.*

1. In a bowl, mix together the steak, soy sauce, sugar, garlic, sesame oil, red pepper flakes, and black pepper, tossing well to combine. Cover and marinate for at least 30 minutes.

2. In a sauté pan over medium-high heat, warm the olive oil. Discard the marinade, add the steak, and sauté for about 2 minutes for medium-rare.

3. Spoon into lettuce leaves, garnish with sesame seeds and scallions, and serve.

HELPFUL HINT Flank or skirt steaks can be a little tough to work with. By marinating them in an acid (such as vinegar) for hours, they will be much more tender.

2 pounds flank or skirt steak, thinly sliced

⅔ cup low-sodium soy sauce

4 tablespoons sugar

6 garlic cloves, minced

3 tablespoons sesame oil

1½ teaspoons red pepper flakes

1 teaspoon black pepper

1 tablespoon extra-virgin olive oil

1 small head green leaf lettuce

2 teaspoons toasted sesame seeds

2 scallions, thinly sliced

Rib Eye Steak and Roasted Potatoes with Garlic Butter

SERVES 4 | PREP TIME: 5 MIN | COOK TIME: 25 MIN

GLUTEN-FREE / NUT-FREE

This recipe will result in a beautiful medium-rare steak. If you like yours cooked a bit more, give it another minute or two per side. If you prefer it more rare, reduce the cooking time by 1 minute per side.

1. Season the steaks with salt and pepper.

2. Fill a sauté pan with 1 inch of water, set it over high heat, and bring to a boil.

3. Add the potatoes and cook until they are just fork-tender, 10 to 12 minutes.

4. Drain and transfer the potatoes to a bowl.

5. Reduce the heat to medium-high, melt 1½ tablespoons butter in the pan, then add the steak and sear for 3 minutes. Flip the steak over and sear for an additional 3 minutes.

6. Transfer the steak to a plate and cover loosely with aluminum foil.

4 (8-ounce) rib eye steaks, at room temperature

Salt and black pepper

½ pound baby potatoes, quartered

5½ tablespoons butter, divided

3 garlic cloves, minced

7. Add the remaining 4 tablespoons butter, as well as the garlic and cooked potatoes, to the sauté pan and cook until nicely browned, about 6 minutes.

8. Serve the steaks alongside the potatoes.

IN SEASON NOW This dish pairs well with a classic Caesar salad. But if you want something like green beans, simply add them to the water when you're cooking the potatoes the first time. They'll be done in no time.

Classic Beef Bourguignon

SERVES 4 | PREP TIME: 20 MIN | COOK TIME: 2 HOURS

DAIRY-FREE / NUT-FREE / WORTH THE WAIT

What could be better than crispy bacon, hearty chunks of beef, and earthy mushrooms in a rich brown gravy? Just a great glass of red wine and a good bread to go with it. Save this one for a quiet Sunday afternoon when you really have the time to enjoy it.

1. Preheat the oven to 350°F.

2. In a large Dutch oven over medium-high heat, cook the bacon until crispy. Remove it from the Dutch oven and drain on a paper towel–lined plate.

3. Season the beef with salt and pepper. Brown the beef in batches in the bacon fat, being careful not to crowd the pan. Set the browned beef on a plate. Drain off the fat into a heat-proof container, leaving behind 2 tablespoons. Add fat back to the Dutch oven if it becomes dry while sautéing the vegetables.

4. Sauté the carrot until slightly tender, then add in the mushrooms and cook for 3 minutes or until slightly softened. Add in the garlic and cook for 30 seconds. Add the flour and stir into the vegetables.

5. Deglaze the pan with the wine, scraping the browned bits from the bottom of the pan. Return the beef and the bacon to the pan.

½ pound bacon, roughly chopped

2 pounds cubed beef chuck

Salt and black pepper

3 carrots, sliced

1 pound cremini or button mushrooms, quartered

3 garlic cloves, minced

2 tablespoons all-purpose flour

1 (750 ml) bottle dry red wine

2 cups low-sodium beef stock

1 tablespoon tomato paste

1 teaspoon dried thyme

1 bay leaf

1 pound frozen pearl onions

6. Pour in the beef stock, tomato paste, thyme, bay leaf, and onion.

7. Cover and bake for 90 minutes, or until the beef is fork-tender. Season to taste with additional salt and pepper, remove the bay leaf, and serve.

HELPFUL HINT Few dishes are as mouthwateringly delicious as beef Bourguignon—made famous by that culinary pioneer Julia Child. She was famous for saying that the beef had to be good and dry before you try to sauté it, otherwise it never browns properly. Simply pat it dry with a paper towel before seasoning it.

Shepherd's Pie

SERVES 4 | PREP TIME: 15 MIN | COOK TIME: 30 MIN

GLUTEN-FREE / NUT-FREE

The British aren't necessarily known for their culinary prowess, but throw those thoughts out the window. This delicious comfort food combination is definitely the exception. Make two of these and freeze one for later.

1. Set an oven rack in the position closest to the broiler. Preheat the broiler.

2. Place the potatoes in a skillet and add enough water to cover them. Put the skillet over high heat, bring to a boil, and cook until they are fork-tender.

3. Drain and season with salt and pepper to taste. Add in the butter and mash the potatoes. Add in the milk and continue mashing until creamy. Set the potatoes aside in a bowl.

4. Reheat the skillet over high and brown the ground beef, 6 minutes.

5. Add in the carrot and cook for 2 minutes. Add in the onion and mushrooms and cook until softened, 5 minutes. Add in the garlic and cook for 30 seconds.

6. Pour in the peas, heavy cream, and sour cream, stirring well to mix. Season with additional salt and pepper, as well as the thyme and cayenne. Top with the mashed potatoes.

7. Place the entire skillet under the broiler for 4 minutes, or until slightly browned.

VARIATION If you prefer not to use ground beef, you could also substitute ground lamb, chicken, or turkey—or even try a meatless version.

3 russet potatoes, peeled and cubed

Salt and black pepper

4 tablespoons butter

¼ cup milk or cream

1 pound ground beef

2 carrots, diced

1 onion, diced

1 (8-ounce) package mushrooms, sliced

3 garlic cloves, minced

1 cup peas

1 cup heavy cream

½ cup sour cream

1 teaspoon dried thyme

⅛ teaspoon cayenne pepper

Guinness Corned Beef and Cabbage

SERVES 4 | PREP TIME: 5 MIN | COOK TIME: 1 HOUR 40 MIN

DAIRY-FREE / GLUTEN-FREE / NUT-FREE / WORTH THE WAIT

Cabbage is one of winter's star vegetables, and its hardy nature was made for this dish. Also, I bet you have all of the ingredients it takes to make your own pickling spice mix: mustard seed, allspice, coriander, cloves, ginger, bay leaf, and cinnamon are traditional ingredients in this spice blend.

1. Pour the beer and water into the pressure cooker.

2. Place the corned beef, fat-side up, in the pressure cooker. Sprinkle on the pickling spices.

3. Close and lock the lid, closing off the vent, and pressure cook on high for 1 hour 20 minutes. Allow to depressurize naturally.

4. Remove the corned beef. Cover lightly with foil.

5. Place the onion, cabbage, carrots, and potatoes in the pressure cooker. Seal and pressure cook on high for 4 minutes. Quick release the pressure.

6. Slice the corned beef and serve with the vegetables and the juice from the pot.

ALT POT Corned beef was made for a slow cooker. Simply add all of the ingredients to the pot, cover and set on high for 5 hours or low for 8 hours and enjoy the smells. If using a Dutch oven, cover and place the pot in a 350°F oven for 2 hours.

1 (12-ounce) bottle Guinness stout

2 cups water

1 (3- to 4-pound) corned beef brisket

2 tablespoons pickling spices

1 onion, thinly sliced

1 small head cabbage, thinly sliced

2 cups baby carrots

3 cups baby potatoes

Short Ribs

SERVES 4 | PREP TIME: 10 MIN | COOK TIME: 55 MIN

GLUTEN-FREE / NUT-FREE

Traditionally cooked for hours, making this in a pressure cooker shows how wonderful this appliance is when you can have dinner on the table in an hour or less.

1. Preheat pressure cooker on sauté. Season the short ribs with salt and pepper to taste.

2. Pour the oil in the pressure cooker and brown the ribs until they are well browned on all sides, 10 minutes. Add the onion to the pot and cook until it is softened, about 4 minutes. Add in the garlic, thyme, and bay leaves and cook for 30 seconds. Deglaze with the red wine, letting it cook down until it nearly evaporates.

3. Pour in the stock and vinegar. Place the potatoes in a metal bowl that fits in the pressure cooker on top of the ribs.

4. Close and lock the lid, closing off the vent, and pressure cook on high for 40 minutes. Quick release the pressure.

5. Remove the potatoes. Add the butter to them and mash. Add as much milk as you need to make them creamy. Season to taste.

6 bone-in short ribs (about 4 pounds total)

Salt and black pepper

1 tablespoon extra-virgin olive oil

1 onion, diced

6 garlic cloves, minced

1 teaspoon dried thyme

2 bay leaves

½ cup dry red wine

½ cup low-sodium beef stock

2 tablespoons balsamic vinegar

3 russet potatoes, peeled and quartered

4 tablespoons butter, cut into pieces

¼ cup whole milk

1 tablespoon cornstarch

6. Remove ¼ cup of the liquid from the pot into one of the measuring cups you've already used. Let it cool slightly, then whisk in the cornstarch until there are no lumps. Whisk the slurry into the remaining juices in the pot. Turn the pot back to sauté and whisk until the juices thicken.

7. Season to taste with salt and pepper. Remove the bay leaves and serve the ribs over the mashed potatoes and top with the sauce.

ALT POT Short ribs can also be made in a Dutch oven—but you'll have to forgo the potatoes. Cover the ribs after you've browned them and added the other ingredients. Then finish in a 350°F oven for about 2 hours.

Measurement Conversions

	U.S. STANDARD	U.S. STANDARD (OUNCES)	METRIC (APPROXIMATE)
VOLUME EQUIVALENTS (LIQUID)	2 tablespoons	1 fl. oz.	30 mL
	¼ cup	2 fl. oz.	60 mL
	½ cup	4 fl. oz.	120 mL
	1 cup	8 fl. oz.	240 mL
	1½ cups	12 fl. oz.	355 mL
	2 cups or 1 pint	16 fl. oz.	475 mL
	4 cups or 1 quart	32 fl. oz.	1 L
	1 gallon	128 fl. oz.	4 L
VOLUME EQUIVALENTS (DRY)	⅛ teaspoon	———	0.5 mL
	¼ teaspoon	———	1 mL
	½ teaspoon	———	2 mL
	¾ teaspoon	———	4 mL
	1 teaspoon	———	5 mL
	1 tablespoon	———	15 mL
	¼ cup	———	59 mL
	⅓ cup	———	79 mL
	½ cup	———	118 mL
	⅔ cup	———	156 mL
	¾ cup	———	177 mL
	1 cup	———	235 mL
	2 cups or 1 pint	———	475 mL
	3 cups	———	700 mL
	4 cups or 1 quart	———	1 L
	½ gallon	———	2 L
	1 gallon	———	4 L
WEIGHT EQUIVALENTS	½ ounce	———	15 g
	1 ounce	———	30 g
	2 ounces	———	60 g
	4 ounces	———	115 g
	8 ounces	———	225 g
	12 ounces	———	340 g
	16 ounces or 1 pound	———	455 g

	FAHRENHEIT (F)	CELSIUS (C) (APPROXIMATE)
OVEN TEMPERATURES	250°F	120°C
	300°F	150°C
	325°F	180°C
	375°F	190°C
	400°F	200°C
	425°F	220°C
	450°F	230°C

Recipe Index

Index

P

About the Author

Gwyn Novak is the chef and founder of No Thyme to Cook, Maryland's premier cooking studio, teaching students of all ages the love of food. Gwyn's emphasis is on using locally sourced ingredients to create delicious, yet simple, dishes. She is a graduate of the Baltimore International Culinary College and a member of the International Association of Culinary Professionals, as well as Women Chefs & Restauranteurs. Gwyn has been cooking and writing about food for more than 25 years. She is the author of *How to Cook for Beginners* (2019, Rockridge Press).

CPSIA information can be obtained
at www.ICGtesting.com
Printed in the USA
JSHW021112111020
8648JS00002B/5

9 781647 390051